SpringerBriefs in Business

For further volumes:
http://www.springer.com/series/8860

Ronnie J. Phillips

Rock and Roll Fantasy?

The Reality of Going from Garage Band to Superstardom

Springer

Ronnie J. Phillips
Colorado State University
Fort Collins, CO, USA

ISSN 2191-5482 ISSN 2191-5490 (electronic)
ISBN 978-1-4614-5899-9 ISBN 978-1-4614-5900-2 (eBook)
DOI 10.1007/978-1-4614-5900-2
Springer New York Heidelberg Dordrecht London

Library of Congress Control Number: 2012951330

Printed on acid-free paper

Springer is part of Springer Science+Business Media (www.springer.com)

To the members and faithful fans
of The Penus DeMilo Swing Band

Acknowledgments

First and foremost I would like to thank the Ewing Marion Kauffman Foundation for financial support for this project and especially Bob Litan, Vice President for Research and Policy, for his encouragement.

I have benefited greatly from the work of Tyler Cowen on cultural economics. It was his book *In Praise of Commercial Culture* that first motivated me to pursue my interests in the economics of the music industry. I also thank Zoltan Acs of George Mason University and David Audretsch of Indiana University for their friendship and their path-breaking research on entrepreneurship.

I learned how to play the guitar in the wake of the British Invasion of 1964. I thank my seventh grade math teacher, Gary Duncan, for teaching me how to play the guitar and encouraging me to get a Ph.D.

Though I never gave up my day job, I greatly enjoyed playing in bands. My first rocking teenage combo was The Peer Gents with John "Vinny" DeMore, Harold Lawson, and the late Richard Rogers. My musical tastes were forever influenced by the late A.T. "Bud" Savisky who introduced me to the music of The Fugs and The Mothers of Invention. This led to my greatest joy in music performance with the infamous Penus DeMilo Swing Band during my undergraduate years at The University of Oklahoma. It was the finest collection of insane and creative band-mates ever assembled. When we called Frank Zappa to wish him a Happy Mother's Day in 1971, he was impressed that we had a saxophone player, keyboards, and 14 other people in the band. We were the original proto–punk band—"Cheap Thrills" and "Peggy Sue"—and we definitely had "No Commercial Potential."

I learned a lot from the students I taught in the senior seminar on the music industry at Colorado State University. I would especially like to thank Emily Brophy, Chauncy Bjork, Mike Lopez of the group Gashead, Ben Prytherch of the group Motorhome, and my graduate research assistant, Ian Strachan.

I have been fortunate to know Ken Broad, administrator of the Norman and Vi Petty Estate, and George Tomsco, Stan Lark, and the late Chuck Tharp all members of The Fireballs from Raton, New Mexico. I also benefited greatly from a careful reading of my manuscript by Steve Cassells, an inductee into the Nebraska Rock and Roll Hall of Fame and keyboardist for the The Drivin' Dynamics (which included Randy Meisner, a founding member of The Eagles). I also thank Johnny Mulhair, Johnny Goad, Wally Sanders, Richard Croxdale, Ben Wildavsky, and Ron Stanfield.

Finally, to my wife, Patricia Landy, for her support and to the rest of my family who never thought I could make it in the music industry. They were right.

Abstract and Keywords

Abstract We are in an era where developments in both technology and musical style have coalesced to produce the greatest period of change in the music industry since the invention of recorded sound. Globalization, the Internet, and digital technology are now opening up possibilities for more artists to be innovative and financially successful. But new music requires new ways of doing business. For more artists to be better off requires new business models to replace those that dominated the twentieth century. Integrating insights from economics, management, and intellectual property law, the author explores the dynamics of entrepreneurship and innovation in the music industry, and offers such provocative assessments as these:

- The Beatles might never have broken up if they had the kind of two-tier contracts—as band members and as solo artists—that are common in the music industry today.
- Buddy Holly would likely have avoided his tragic death in a plane crash at age 22 if his 1959 tour had been sponsored by a company like Coca Cola because today's corporatized tours are vastly better financed and organized than the haphazard efforts of the 1950s.
- The economic value of albums by the likes of Elvis and Michael Jackson has risen significantly since their deaths—the ironic by-product of the way their behavior tarnished their own brands while they were alive.
- Diana Ross might never have quit The Supremes if she had known that one-third of the artists in the 1960s who quit the group had charting careers of only 1 year.
- Thomas Edison's invention of the phonograph led to the modern record industry, but he is really the godfather of computer programs like Garageband which have created home recording studios.
- The collapse of the Soviet Union threatened the sound of rock and roll, but an American entrepreneur saved the day.

Keywords Artists, ASCAP, *Billboard*, Copyright, Entrepreneurship, Innovation, Intellectual property, Music business, Music industry, Royalty

Prologue: Who Killed Buddy Holly?

The heart of a capitalist economy is the incessant creation of something new—this can be ideas, goods, or services. But when something new is created that invariably means that something old must disappear. This process of the emergence of the new and the demise of the old was labeled "creative destruction" by the great twentieth century economist Joseph Schumpeter. He believed that this was the essence of a capitalist economy and what differentiated it from other economic systems. The agent of this change is the individual. It is the entrepreneur who takes the risk in creating something new. The turmoil in the music industry today can best be understood within Schumpeter's process of creative destruction. Digital technology and the Internet have made the business model for music that emerged in the early twentieth century obsolete for the twenty-first.

The premise of this book is that we are in an era where developments in both technology and musical style have coalesced to produce the greatest period of change in the music industry since the invention of recorded sound. Technology has always benefited the music industry, but the way of doing business in the industry is slow to change when technology changes. This is true today with the Internet and digital technology. The industry is just beginning to catch up to the technological developments. Globalization, the Internet, and digital technology are now opening up possibilities for more artists to be innovative and financially successful. But new music requires new ways of doing business. For more artists to be better off requires new business models to replace those that dominated the twentieth century. This book draws on the past to help understand the changes to the music business that will occur in the future.

One often hears the view expressed that the musicians who create music, and perhaps artists in general, do not receive adequate monetary compensation for their contributions to the well-being of society. The image of the "starving artist" is brought to mind. But what about the wealth of hip-hop artists such as Snoop Dogg and Jay-Z? What is the key to their success? The answer is that they have been innovative in their music and in their approach to the music business and have successfully gone against the prevailing way of operating a music business enterprise.

In a word, they are entrepreneurs—those who bring innovations to the marketplace. When one talks of success in the music industry, what usually comes to mind is making it as a superstar: The Beatles, Madonna, Michael Jackson, for example. However, changes in the industry due to technology force changes both in the business model and in the definition of success. As the innovative and entrepreneurial artist Amanda Palmer told *Billboard*: "People need to get out of this old mind-set about fame being some sort of a game you can win and look at ways for musicians to make sustainable, middle class incomes." In 2012, Palmer utilized kickstarter.com to fund her new album—raising over $1,000,000 from over 10,000 people.

This dramatic change in the music industry has occurred over more than a century but has accelerated in the past two decades. With the rise of recorded music in the early twentieth century, the record company replaced the sheet music company as the central business organization in the music industry. The record company that evolved over the twentieth century now appears to be in its waning years. Consequently it is essential now more than ever that musicians understand both the creative and business sides of music. We are now in a transition period where these new models are being forged and the old way of life in the recorded music industry is disappearing.

This conflict between the new ways and the old ways of operating has always characterized the music industry and especially the period of rock and roll which is the focus of this book. One such innovative artist whom I use in the chapters that follow as an example of this conflict between old and new is Buddy Holly. February 3, 2009, marked the 50th anniversary of "the day the music died." That day, immortalized by Don Mclean in the song "American Pie," Buddy Holly, J.P. "The Big Bopper" Richardson, and Ritchie Valens were killed near Clear Lake, Iowa, in the crash of a small plane along with their 21-year-old pilot, Roger Peterson. Strapped for cash, in the midst of a lawsuit and with a pregnant wife, Holly began the long, cold tour through the Midwest in January. Holly chartered a plane so that he and his band members (Waylon Jennings and Tommy Allsup) could arrive sooner at the next gig in order to recuperate from the ill effects of a tour by bus in the middle of winter. Jennings gave up his seat to the Big Bopper, and Tommy Allsup lost his seat in a coin toss with Valens [98]. Bad weather and an inexperienced pilot were the immediate blame for the crash, but in a larger sense it could be attributed to the economics of the early rock and roll industry.

Buddy Holly: Innovative Artist and Businessman

Holly's musical style and songwriting were influential on the 1960s—a period that is often regarded as one of the most innovative in terms of musical style. But Holly's musical style went side by side with the business organization of his band, his songwriting, and his contracts. His career also highlights problems with the organization of touring in the 1950s and the question of how to keep an artist's memory and music alive after one's death. There are many aspects of Holly's approach to the business of music that are now emerging as part of the new and innovative ways that musicians are garnering a greater share of the money pie. For Holly, new technology and the innovations surrounding the advent of rock and roll were helpful for his career, but the prevailing organization and operation of the music business ultimately were detrimental and contributed to his untimely death. Holly was one of the first to break the shackles of the Tin Pan Alley business model that had shaped American popular music since the turn of the twentieth century. It is only now—more than five decades after Holly's death—that we are finally seeing the widespread viability of new business models that make the old way of doing business in the industry obsolete.

Holly was one of the first singer-songwriters. The Rolling Stones' first single release in the USA in 1964 was the Holly song "Not Fade Away." Holly also had a great impact on John Lennon and Paul McCartney who took the singer–songwriter model to its penultimate development. At the time of his death, Holly was planning on expanding his singer–songwriter talents to producing records and creating his own music publishing company. Though virtually no one was a singer–songwriter–producer in 1959, today it is the model for many artists, especially those in the rap and hip-hop genre.

Some put the blame for Holly's death on his producer and manager Norman Petty who had allegedly withheld royalty payments to Holly. The Buddy Holly–Norman Petty relationship was one of the earliest and clearest representations of the changed nature of producing music. Prior to the Rock and Roll Era, there was a fairly rigid division of labor in the production of music. The songwriter, the Artists & Repertoire (A & R) person, the producer, and the performer were all separate individuals. This changed in the 1950s and technology had a lot to do with the changes. The producer became someone who played an important role in creating a hit song and the recording studio became an instrument for producing the sound.

Singer-songwriters can earn both mechanical and performance royalties on the songs they have written and recorded. Mechanical royalties are tied to record sales, and performance royalties are paid whenever the song is performed live. Most of Holly's songs were cowritten with Petty. This was unusual for the 1950s, but today is quite common and even the standard practice in some genres. Holly earned 5 cents per record in mechanical royalties and if he had had a standard arrangement, then he would have paid his producer a fixed amount, say 1 cent per record sold. Petty was an innovative producer who charged a fixed fee per recording rather than the hourly rate that was the standard then and now and did not take a fixed payment from mechanical royalties. To compensate for his risks and to recognize his contribution to creating the song, Petty was often listed as a cowriter of the songs he produced, and the songs were published by his music publishing company, Nor-Va-Jak Music. Songwriting and music publishing were lucrative, but as a cowriter, Buddy Holly shared 50 % of the performance royalties from The Crickets' first hit "That'll Be the Day" with his cowriters, Jerry Allison and Petty (each receiving 16 and two-thirds percent). The other 50 % of the royalties went to music publishing companies Peer-Southern and the Petty-owned Nor-Va-Jak. No doubt Petty took risks as the producer and deserved compensation for his efforts, but his percentage of performance royalties was greater than Holly's and the question is whether this was more than Petty deserved. Those who would defend Petty's greater share would point to the fact that Holly and the Crickets did not produce any hits before they recorded with Petty in his Clovis, New Mexico, studio. The accepted split between the songwriter and music publisher, which was a leftover from the Tin Pan Alley days when sheet music publishers employed song pluggers to help sell music to the public, created a problem in the relationship between Holly and Petty.

But it is also the case that Holly's contractual relationships with Petty were definitely not all detrimental to Holly. There were separate contracts for Holly as a solo performer and as a member of The Crickets. This was another innovation for this period and is more common today for artists such as Wil.i.am who releases solo songs and performs with the group the Black Eyed Peas. Had The Beatles had separate contracts as solo and group performers, this might have prevented the breakup of the band. Because the technology of the long-playing 33 rpm record (LP) limited the amount of music that could be recorded on a single album and because songwriting royalties were an important source of income, George Harrison and Ringo Starr were both limited in the number of songs they wrote that could be on the album. That Harrison had a lot of songs that he could not get on Beatles' albums is evidenced by his release of a three-record set as his initial solo album. What if The Beatles could have continued to record and perform as a group and yet each individual member could have made solo recordings? The band might have continued on for many more years, as have The Rolling Stones who were major competitors to The Beatles in the 1960s.

Buddy Holly's band organization was also highly influential on the 1960s. Holly, who played lead guitar and sang vocals, was one of the first to use a drummer, rhythm guitar, and bass guitar. This band was different because it used fewer skilled musicians who could not read music and had less equipment when compared with the Big Bands of the 1930s and 1940s. Rather than reading their parts from sheet music, the other members of the band—drummer, bass player, and rhythm guitar—for the most wrote their own parts around the melody. The rap groups of the 1980s took this innovation even further in using even fewer members in the group who could not read music but rather they rapped to a beat. The equipment needed for the rap group was also less than that of the early rock bands: a public address (PA) system, a microphone, and a turntable.

Artists have also helped promote innovation in the equipment they used. Holly was an innovator in recording sound. His father owned a tile company, and Holly and his father and brother created a tiled recording room away from the main studio in order to create a natural echo sound in Holly's voice on records. But unfortunately for Holly and others in the early years of rock and roll, the technology to support quality sounding live performances with electrified guitars was not available in the 1950s. There were no monitor speakers, and the vocals were often inputted into old vacuum-tube technology public address (PA) systems that were set up originally for non-musical use. Performers could not hear their own vocals nor could they hear other members of the group. The composition of the band was ahead of the technology available, but it led to attempts by sound experts and musicians in the 1960s, like Neil Young, who eventually were able to produce adequate monitor speaker setups. It is not surprising that there are no high-quality recordings of live performances in the 1950s. It is not until Woodstock in 1969 that monitor speakers were used so that performers could hear themselves and a high-quality recording could be produced. Today, wireless monitors are inserted in the ear of the performer who can now hear all instruments and vocals.

Ultimately, it was the economics of touring in the late 1950s that resulted in the tragic death of Holly and the others. A rock and roll concert tour of artists with charting songs, as was the Winter Dance Party, was an innovation. Often touring in the 1950s was a cost associated with record promotion that had to be paid for by the artists out of their earnings on sales of the record. What artists received from touring was sometimes quite small after costs were deducted from their future mechanical royalties. Those tours that were not organized by the record companies to help promote record sales had to produce a profit for the company that organized the tour. Unfortunately, the venues and the means of traveling to the venues were not adequate to support the kind of touring exemplified by the Winter Dance Party. The Big Bands of the 1930s and 1940s performed in ballrooms designed for their performance, i.e., large bands with no electrified instruments and a P.A. system only for the single singer. The Big Bands also traveled to these different venues via an extensive passenger rail network in the USA at the time. For the rock and rollers, these tours were via buses, which were definitely not luxurious in the 1950s, and on two-lane roads since the Interstate highway system did not begin until 1956. Many, if not most, tours were very inefficient in the 1950s and this contributed to Holly's decision to pay for travel for himself and his band via a small private plane.

Corporate sponsorship is the norm in present-day touring and rather than being a cost of production that is deducted from record royalties, it is instead often a more important source of revenue for the artists than recording. Consider the fact that major artists such as Madonna have forsaken recording companies altogether to instead sign with touring companies like Live Nation. There were also no "360 deals" in the 1950s as there are today that specify a sharing of most sources of revenue (merchandise and so on) between the artist and the label.

Not only were Holly's financial rewards limited in the 1950s by all of these factors, but after his death, Holly's memory and stature in the music industry languished until The Beatles brought new interest in his music by covering Holly songs. Norman Petty did attempt to keep Holly's music alive by innovative efforts at creating new recordings of Holly in the studio with a new backup band, The Fireballs. Though the success was modest, the production of new music with dead artists has become widely accepted as a legitimate endeavor. Holly's music and reputation have remained more than 50 years after his death due to the efforts of Paul McCartney who purchased the publishing rights to Holly's Nor-Va-Jak music songs in the late 1970s. As an example, an original recording of a relatively obscure Holly–Petty song "Take Your Time" was used in a Visa commercial in 2007.

The Shape of Things to Come

Buddy Holly's life and career are illustrative of the problems all musicians face and of the decisions they must make about their music careers. This book first examines the organization of a performing group or band, songwriting, contracts, touring, and death. It also discusses whether there are innovative periods in rock music and the characteristics of innovative artists. The interaction between artists and inventor that has produced innovation in technology is also discussed. Finally, the Internet and digital technology offer the promise that more musicians will be better compensated in the future than they have in the past. Though it appears now that musicians must focus more attention on the business aspects of their craft, the future also will likely see new types of jobs created as the new business models emerge.

Many books have been written about the coming changes in the music industry. It also seems that every rock star has written or cowritten the story of their rise to fame and fortune. The present book is written with an eye on history, but a recognition that the way in which we produce and consume music is undergoing radical change. The focus is on the entrepreneurial aspects of the industry that have been the key to change and innovation. Rather than relying on anecdotal stories, I have used data collected from *Billboard* and other sources to understand where music has been and where it may be going. Ironically, the changes that are now occurring in the industry may lead us back to a new role for the live music that many thought was endangered by technology at the turn of the twentieth century. It may also be that everybody can be a rock and roll star—at least for Andy Warhol's 15 min. Rock and Roll is here to stay.

Contents

List of Figures

List of Tables

Chapter 1
So You Want to Be a Rock and Roll Star?

There aren't many "one man bands" anymore. There is a physical limit—two hands, two feet, one mouth—that makes it difficult to play more than two or three instruments at a time. It also requires skill in playing multiple instruments simultaneously [90]. However, the drawback of a multiple member band is that the band members must cooperate to produce the sound and also decide how to divide up any income earned. The music produced by a band is of necessity a joint product. The reason music is produced by a duet, trio, quartet or orchestra is presumably because you cannot get the same music output without the combination of instruments and performers. The problem of remuneration for each member is also an important aspect of a band. Since the singer cannot perform the song unless someone also plays drums or guitar, most rock groups have begun with a reward structure that compensates every member with an equal share of the band's income. This is where the trouble begins in keeping a group together. Though each is necessary to produce the sound, some members may view themselves as more necessary than others. If good drummers are hard to find, then drummers will have to receive a greater share of the band's revenue. If it is the lead singer who provides the unique sound of the band, he or she will have to be given additional compensation in some manner.

In this chapter, I examine 1960s musical groups and evaluate how well they did in terms of chart success and longevity. I then discuss how the rap and hip-hop artists redefined the rock group in the 1980s and laid the basis for a new business model that has worked well for compensating artists.

1.1 The Economic Organization of a Rock and Roll Band

When rock and roll bands emerged in the 1950s, they were quite different from the bands that preceded them. Marching bands originated with the military and were used to help direct troop movements on the battlefield. By the early twentieth century, they could be found in many colleges and universities. They were composed of numerous brass and woodwind instruments and led by a baton major. While big cities

R.J. Phillips, *Rock and Roll Fantasy?: The Reality of Going from Garage Band to Superstardom*, SpringerBriefs in Business 35, DOI 10.1007/978-1-4614-5900-2_1,

had orchestras playing classical music, in the latter part of the nineteenth century and the early part of the twentieth century, many small towns had bands composed of local citizens playing popular songs on brass and woodwind instruments. This era was depicted in the musical *The Music Man* which was produced in the 1950s.

In the 1980 movie, *The Blues Brothers*, Jake and Elwood must put their band back together in order to perform a concert to raise money to keep their childhood parochial school open. The band members had scattered since the band broke up after Jake went to prison. Most of the band members have found day jobs except for five members who are booked in a steady gig at a Holiday Inn lounge under the name Murph and the Magictones. When Jake and Elwood's arrival at the concert is delayed, the Blues Brothers Band transforms into a Big Band featuring the school janitor (played by the great Cab Calloway) and they perform the 1930s classic "Minnie the Moocher." It makes for a great scene in the movie as the band plays behind podiums, and it preserves on film a reprieve of Calloway's 1930s hit. It was a fitting tribute to the Big Band era, but it was the rock era that helped put these Big Bands out of business. There is a world of difference between the organization of a Big Band and a rock and roll group.

The Big Bands of the 1930s and 1940s included as many as 30 or more musicians and were led by a conductor or prominent player and were usually referred to as orchestras. Hence, you had Benny Goodman and his Orchestra, Cab Calloway and his Orchestra, Fred Waring and the Pennsylvanians, and so on. To get into a Big Band you auditioned and if you got in you were paid a regular salary. The typical band member did not write the music and only performed one function: play the saxophone, for example. Big Bands made lots of recordings and the members of the band were paid to perform on these records, most likely at some established union hourly wage. Members of Big Bands were paid according to their skill as a musician and probably according to the supply and demand for their particular instrument. Big Bands would sometimes feature singers such as Doris Day or Harriet Hilliard. The musicians in the Big Bands had varying levels of music education but since the bands played from music scores, everyone had to be able to read music. Competition could be quite fierce to be in the best bands and prominent artists and singers often left one group to join another. The identity of the band, however, was tied closely to the orchestra leader and not the individual members.

In many ways, the rock band was the antithesis of the Big Band. Bill Haley was an early innovator with his band the Comets. This group's single "Rock Around the Clock" marks the beginning of the rock era when the song charted after appearing in the movie *The Blackboard Jungle* in 1955. This group is a transition group from Big Bands to the rock bands in the sense that there were seven members in the band. It included a lead guitar, saxophone, steel guitar, piano, stand-up bass guitar, drums and Haley on rhythm guitar and vocals. This group was a modification of the country swing bands such as Bob Wills and his Texas Playboys whose instrumentation varied, but included fiddles and a drummer. The latter was not standard for country and western bands since bluegrass music groups such as Bill Monroe's Bluegrass Boys used all acoustic instruments without any electronic amplification. Indeed, drums were forbidden for live performances at the Grand Ole Opry in Nashville.

Buddy Holly and the Crickets were one of the first groups to include a lead guitar, rhythm guitar, bass guitar, and drums. This band composition became standard in the late 1950s and was solidified by influential instrumental groups like The Fireballs and surf music groups like The Ventures who had the same composition in the early 1960s. A keyboard player sometimes supplemented this four-member band so that the typical 1960s rock group included four or five members. It is with the arrival of The Beatles in the early 1960s that there is an explosion of "garage bands"—so called because that was about the only place for teenage rock bands to practice [148].

The 1960s are considered by many to be the heyday of the rock group: The Beatles, The Rolling Stones, The Beach Boys and so on. If you look at the top 100 singles in 1965, two-thirds were by groups. Though there were groups in the 1950s, many of these were vocal groups (The Coasters, The Platters, and so on) that used studio musicians on their recordings and touring. There were also vocal groups in the 1960s such as the female vocal groups The Shirelles and The Supremes who also used studio musicians. Studio players were paid by the hour, were competent and versatile musicians, who played on many recordings and often went on tour with the artists. Unlike the members of the typical group in the early days of rock and roll, most of the studio musicians could read music from lead sheets.

The inability of many rock and rollers to read sheet music led Big band members to view rock musicians as something less than professional musicians. Unlike the Big Bands, the rock and roll bands did not play from music scores. As the rock era unfolded, and Big Bands declined, there was an increase in unemployment of the skilled Big Band musicians and necessarily resentment. Many of the rock and roll era musicians had little formal musical training and often could not read sheet music at all. This was true of The Beatles and many other groups. Occasionally, however, band members could have some musical training, but in general, being in a rock and roll band did not require the ability to read sheet music. In economic terms, the level of investment in music human capital was much lower for rock and roll bands.

The four or five piece rock and roll band was made possible by improvements in amplification of sound and the invention of the flat body electric guitar by Adolph Rickenbacher with his "frying pan" guitar in 1930 and especially Leo Fender who introduced the Broadcaster/Telecaster guitar in 1949. These technological innovations, which are discussed in more detail in a later chapter, made a small band possible. Without an amplifier, acoustic guitars could be miked, but there was a problem with both sound quality and electronic feedback. The Beatles were the first band to play to very large venues and in order to do so, greater amplification of guitars, drums, and vocals were needed. The Beatles used British-made Vox amplifiers for their instruments. Unfortunately, as The Beatles video recorded performance at Shea Stadium makes clear, it was impossible for the performers to hear themselves because monitor speakers were not used until the late 1960s.

One can think of the rock band as a group in which each member shares the costs and the benefits of being in the group with the other members [35]. Though presumably the sound of both Big Band and rock bands required that each musician work together, the cooperative nature of a rock and roll band is fundamentally different from that of the Big Bands. In most rock bands, the income generated by the band's performance is divided equally among the members unlike the Big Band members who were paid wages. It might be expected that if individual rock band members had problems with this cooperative type of economic organization, they might quit the band or ask for some form of reorganization. Often the lead singer or the main songwriter would ask for some differing compensation scheme or more prominent visibility in the group's name. This problem was especially evident in the early days of rock and roll when a group that starts out with a name that makes individuals anonymous, such as The Animals, becomes Eric Burdon and the Animals. Even for groups that do not add the name of a band member to the band's name, it is often the case that some members become better known or are assumed to be greater contributors to the success of the band than others. Thus it may be the case that the lead singer often becomes the one most recognized by the fans—like Mick Jagger or Jim Morrison—and the drummer and bass player are in some sense viewed as making less of a contribution to the band's sound. However, because of the cooperative nature of production in a rock band, the lead singer could not produce the band's sound without the rest of the members of the band. As noted, the division of labor within the band helps it to produce the music efficiently [35]. It was also clearly the case that, at least initially, Mick Jagger was not the leader of the band in the same sense that Cab Calloway was the leader who could hire and fire members. The big bands were not cooperatives, but small proprietor businesses.

There have been groups that have sought to reconcile the problem of compensating band members equitably even though they make unequal contributions to the production of music. For example, even though someone might be the "star" of the group, they would recognize that without the group, they might not be a "star." If the alternative is the uncertain future of a solo artist, then it might be possible to make compensation arrangements to keep the group together and everyone is better off. One group from the 1980s that sought from the beginning to find a unique solution to this dilemma was the British group Spandau Ballet [24]. They formed a company called Marbelow Ltd. that received all of the band's recording and performance income, and this was divided equally among the five band members and their manager. The songwriter for the group, Gary Kemp, received his publishing income separately but instructed the publisher to pay half of the royalties to Marbelow Ltd. The reason to do this is the recognition that the band had contributed in some way to songwriting. This setup is depicted in Fig. 1.1.

Instead of receiving 100% of the publishing income due him, Kemp received a little less than 60%. This was a verbal agreement and did not appear to cause problems until after the group broke up and in the 1990s three members of the group sought to obtain more songwriting royalties. Because this was not a written contract, their claims for additional songwriting royalties were rejected. This also rejects the view that was implicit in their verbal contract that they had in fact made a contribution to song creation. In a later case, the three members also tried to get use of the band's name, but they lost this case as well. However, by late 2009, the band members had decided to reunite for a reunion tour.

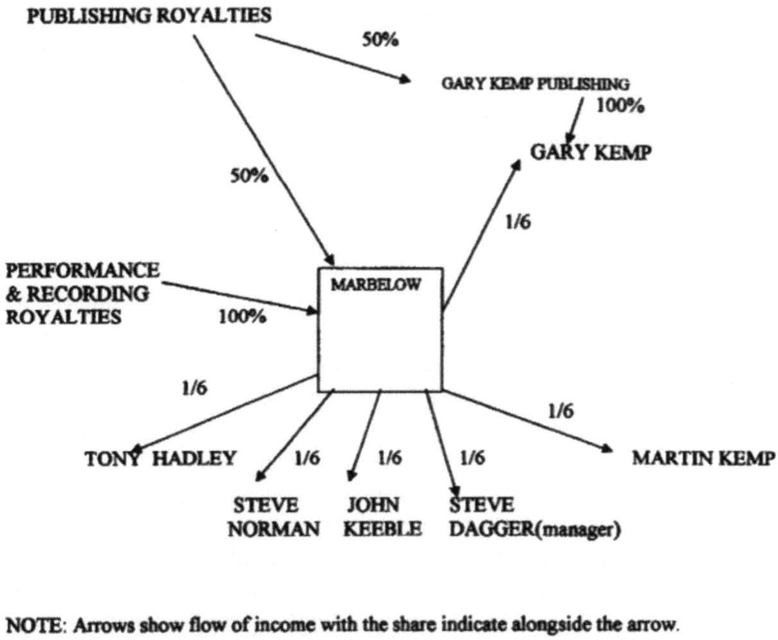

Fig. 1.1 Payment structure of Spandau Ballet income. *Source*: Cameron 2006 [24]

1.2 We're Putting the Band Together!

There are many stories of how bands were put together in the 1950s and 1960s. Most groups came together in one of the following three ways: (1) they met as friends and decided to start a band (Beatles, Rolling Stones, Doors); (2) the band was assembled by a third party, perhaps a record company (The Monkees); (3) the leader of the band hired musicians for a salary (Frank Zappa or Chuck Berry who let the local promoter hire his backup band). A typical story of putting a band together is two of the main members of the band met when they were relatively young and just as they are getting into music. Mick Jagger and Keith Richards met on a train while Jagger was attending the London School of Economics. Paul McCartney met John Lennon when the latter was already playing in a group. The groups were usually formed around a common interest, perhaps of a certain artist. What was typical was that many groups started out as just friends, but there was considerable shifting around until the best musicians at each instrument gravitated toward being in one group. This was the case with The Beatles who had several members before the four members jelled as a group. Pete Best was famous for being kicked out of The Beatles and replaced by Ringo Starr. Who was the better drummer? It is hard to say, but Pete Best did not have much success in the music industry after he left The Beatles.

In the 1960s, inspired by the British invasion, hoards of teenagers (mostly guys, but with a girl singer sometimes) formed rock and roll bands in the USA.

Typically, the band was formed among a group of friends or acquaintances and nearly all had no prior training on how to play the guitar or drums. Because music education was still an important part of the public schools in the 1960s, there were many teenagers who had some exposure to music, though not necessarily to playing rock and roll music. Following The Beatles model, the bands typically included a lead guitar, a rhythm guitar, a bass guitar, and drums. Sometimes there was a fifth member who was a singer or else those playing the instruments also sang. The bands mostly did "covers" of popular tunes, but frequently also tried their hand at writing original songs.

My junior high school band was called "The Peer Gents." We thought it was a nice variant on the Peer Gynt Suite by Henrik Ibsen we which we found a reference to while thumbing through an encyclopedia. Three of us played in the school marching band, including our lead guitar player whose father was the band director at our junior high. He had the most musical training. Our bass player was a pretty good singer. Our equipment was purchased from the mail order catalogues of either Montgomery Wards (now defunct) or Sears. I was the second-rhythm guitar player because I had the least musical talent—the right fielder (which I also played) of teenage rock bands. The toughest member of the band to find was the drummer. They seemed to be in short supply. There could be an explanation for this since you really needed a lot of talent to keep on the beat and there were not many drummers in the school band. There was also a larger investment in equipment for the drummer. Cheap guitars and amps were available but not drum sets. In the music mockumentary, *This is Spinal Tap*, the drummer was always changing. Many 1960s garage bands had similar experiences. My band once had to perform at a party without a drummer. What songs did we play? They were cover songs like "House of the Rising Sun" and "Runaway." However, all of the local bands wanted to do original songs as well. Why? Writing songs meant you could do more than just be a cover band and held out the possibility of greater financial success in the future.

The Peer Gents not only sought to write our own songs, but we also enlisted a female singer for some songs. This made the band different from the other groups. These teenage bands were really start-up firms, but with a very minimum of initial financial investment. Our parents bought us guitars and amps. Some local groups were started in anticipation of greater things—a record contract and touring, but most were started to attract girls and get some prestige for the usually non-athletic oriented males who played in the bands. The garage location also had the added advantage that the teenage girls driving by could hear the band practice and they might stop by to hear a few songs. This often led to shortened practice sessions.

Few, if any, of these teenage garage bands had a business plan for long-term success. My band certainly didn't. This did not mean that there were no changes in the members playing in the band. Your best friend might be a great guy, but that did not necessarily mean that he could learn how to play the bass guitar. The first lesson for the band members was that in order to sound good, cooperation and practice were required. Those without the discipline to practice might end up as the guy who lugged the equipment around to the gigs.

1.3 Survival on the *Billboard* Hot 100

Given the ad hoc nature of forming many of the groups, how well did they do in terms of longevity? Let's start with the 232 groups that made the *Billboard* Hot 100 charts in the 1960s. Though most of these groups first charted in the period 1960–1969, twenty first charted in the 1950s. Also, some of the groups had their greatest success after the 1960s. The first thing to examine is what might be called survival rates for these groups. This is analogous to, though not identical with, measures of survival for new business establishments in a variety of industries that is derived from data collected by the Bureau of Labor Statistics. The group's start begins when it first makes the charts and ends the last year the group makes the charts. A group that charted in 1961 and 1965 only would be considered to have a charting career length of 5 years, for example, even if it had no charting songs from 1962 to 1964. Few groups could chart consistently year after year. Even The Beatles and Elvis Presley never charted more than 4 years in a row, though both had careers considerably longer. Obviously, the measure of career length I use is not the year the group actually started performing, nor the year they broke up. The Rolling Stones formed in 1962 and are still together today. However, their life on the charts as of 2006 is measured as 40 years — 1964–2003. Obviously you can still be making a living in the music industry and not be on the charts, but making the *Billboard* charts is the most consistent measure of whether or not a band is currently relevant to the contemporary music scene. But there can also be anomalies such as The Tokens who made the charts in 1961 with "The Lion Sleeps Tonight" and again in 1994 when the movie *The Lion King* came out. Using my method, The Tokens are credited with a 34-year career, even though they were not really together as a group during this period. It should be noted though that the group was formed in 1956 and included the prolific singer-songwriter Neil Sedaka who left the group in 1958. Though there weren't that many groups with similar histories, by including The Tokens in the data set we can compare their career with Neil Sedaka who made the decision to go solo.

Figure 1.2 plots the length of the charting career for the 232 bands that charted in the 1960s. Of the 232 groups, 85% were on the charts for at least 2 years, 55% lasted at least 4 years, and 36% lasted 7 years. This compares very well with estimates for new business establishment survival in other industries such as construction or financial services where about two-thirds last at least 2 years, 44% last 4 years, and 31% last 7 years [87] That study also found that the longer you survive, the longer you are likely to survive, which is also true of the 1960s groups. Some caveats to these figures should be noted. First of all, there is some selection bias since all we have are groups that succeeded by making the charts. What we don't know is how many groups formed (like my junior high band) and broke up because they didn't make the charts. The failure rate for these groups would likely be significantly higher and their survival much shorter. How many groups from my hometown of 10,000 population were formed between 1965 and 1969? At least 20. How many made a record? One. How many made the *Billboard* charts? Zero. In fairness, the Bureau of Labor Statistics does not include all

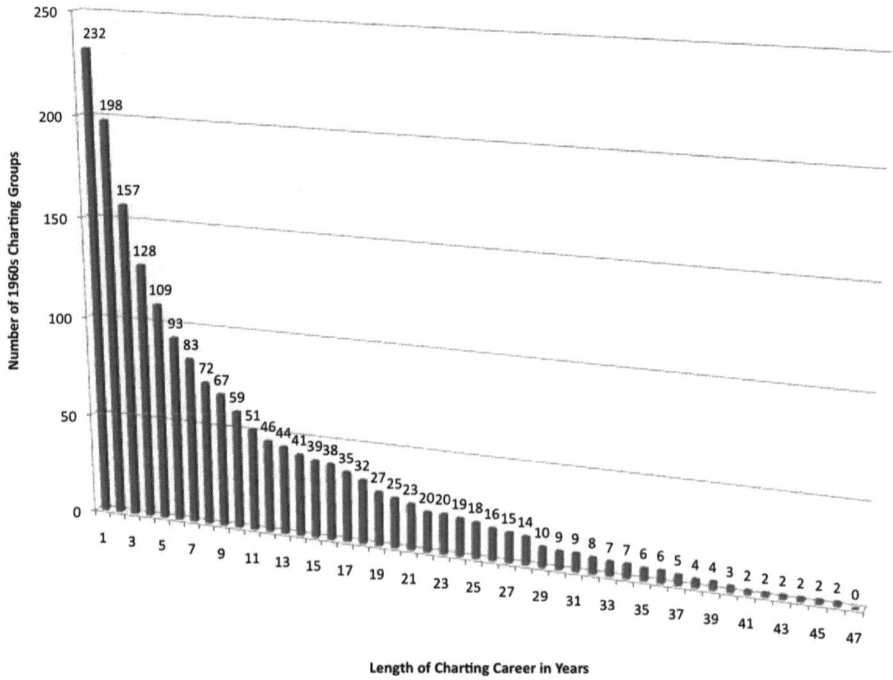

Fig. 1.2 Length of charting career in years for 1960s Charting Rock Groups. *Source*: Whitburn 2006b [152]

startups either, but rather only those who were large enough to be required to pay unemployment insurance.

Of the 232 groups that made the charts between 1960 and 1969, the only major group to survive more or less intact from the 1960s and is still performing today is The Rolling Stones. By the late 1960s, Mick Jagger realized that the contracts they had signed were not ultimately good for the band and the group reorganized their business affairs to gain both greater control over their careers, and most importantly, to retain more of the revenues they were generating for themselves. The cost of the reorganization was that they essentially gave up royalties on many of their songs from the 1960s. Of the 232 groups, about 20% made it into the Rock and Roll Hall of Fame by 2009. Groups accounted for 2,668 charting songs in the period 1960–1969 with the top 10% of groups accounting for 36% of the hits and the top 50% accounting for 85% of the charting songs. The phenomena of "one-hit wonders" is legendary, but only 11 of the bands had only one charting song though over half [126] had only one charting top ten hit.

1.4 Should I Stay or Should I Go?

The cooperative nature of the 1960s rock band and the supposed equality of each member led to problems of continuity of band membership. Big Band musicians left if someone paid them more. Rock band members left if they felt their contribution to the band was not rewarded in proportion to what they were contributing to the group or to what they could make on their own. But was quitting the band and releasing a solo album a good career move? How well did the artists who left a group and went solo survive on the charts when compared to the groups they left? The first thing to note is that artists would be more likely to go solo if their group was successful on the charts. If your group didn't make the charts, a solo career was not a likely option. For groups who did not have someone go solo, only 80% of the 168 groups were still on the charts after 2 years. For groups that had someone go solo, 98% of the 64 groups were still on the charts after 2 years and 80% were on the charts after 4 years. But how did those who went solo do on the charts when compared with the groups they left? Fig. 1.3 plots the survival rates on the *Billboard* Hot 100 for groups that had at least one member who went solo and the survival rates for those 83 artists who went solo. It is clear that the decision to go solo resulted in a much shorter length of survival on the charts. Only 70% of the solo artists were on the charts for 2 years or longer. After 6 years, 70% of the groups who had someone go solo were still on the charts, but only 51% of the solo artists were still on the charts. However, artists who had solo careers that lasted more than 4 years, survived at a higher rate than the groups who did not have anyone go solo. This indicates perhaps that there was some advantage in terms of career length to having been in a group if you survived for 4 years. Examples of those who left their groups and went solo are all four of The Beatles, Eric Clapton, Steve Winwood, and Diana Ross. Table 1.1 lists the top 30 artists who left groups and went solo.

Though as a whole, the survival rates were lower for solo artists than the groups they left, many artists did very well with solo careers. Why were they so successful? Cher was successful because she was really the prominent singer in the duo with Sonny Bono. Carlos Santana benefited from using his name for the group's name, something other artists such as Van Halen and Alice Cooper have also done. One thing is clear is that many of those who were successful solo artists were also songwriters. While groups were important in the 1960s, it also is the beginning of the singer/songwriter's rise to prominence in the music industry.

1.5 Reunion Tours

The previous section discussed the length of the chart career for 1960s groups, but this does not mean the groups stopped touring. The late Chuck Tharp of The Fireballs once told me that the difference between music in the 1960s and today was that it

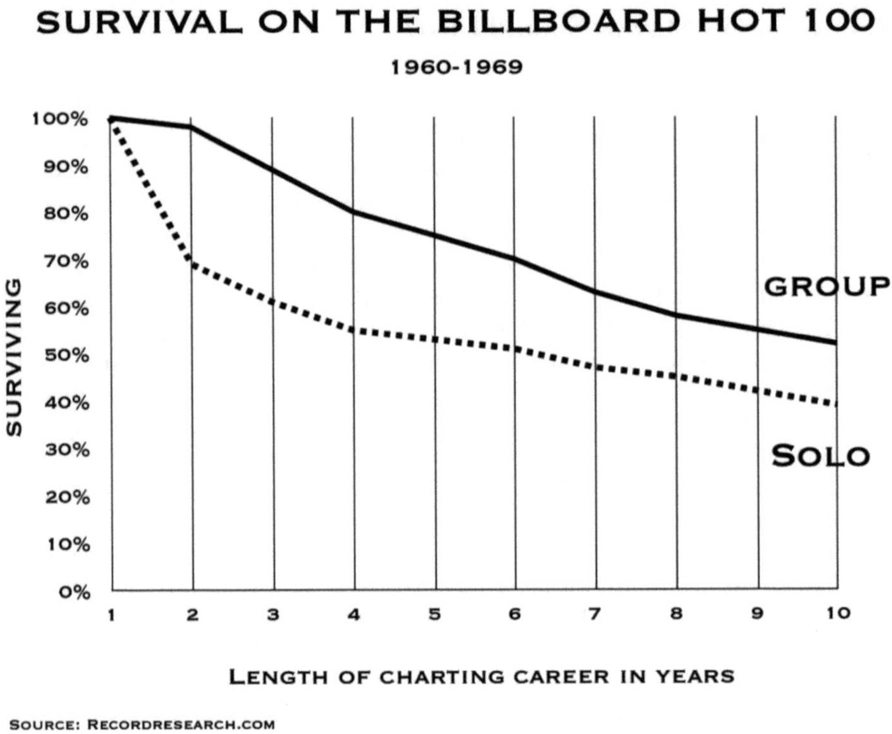

Fig. 1.3 Survival rates for 1960s groups and artists who left the groups and went solo. *Source*: Whitburn 2006b [152]

was the song that was important in the 1960s and not the artist who performed the song. If this is true, it should bode well for reunion tours for 1950s and 1960s groups. The reason is that if you were less focused on who the artists were and more enamored with the song, then you should be more excited about hearing the songs than seeing the original performers. When baby boomers go to see Paul McCartney, they know it's not going to be The Beatles, but they will still get to hear many of the classic Lennon–McCartney songs. The success of Paul McCartney is in part due to the fact that he has a large back catalogue of songs his fans want to hear, even though he is still writing new music. Would McCartney's tours be as successful if he refused to play any Beatles' songs and instead only played his new music? Highly unlikely.

Many of the 1950s and 1960s groups are still touring in some form or other. The Rolling Stones are the prime example. How many original members of the band are there in the Stones today? Three. They are Mick Jagger, Keith Richards, and Charlie Watts. The original lead guitar player, Brian Jones died in 1968 and the original bass player, Bill Wyman, quit touring several years ago. Could the Stones keep touring if any of the remaining three were no longer in the band? Ron Wood, though not an original member of the band, has been with them for over 25 years. For the Stones, they might continue as long as the group contains Jagger and Richards. But what of the other 1960s groups?

Table 1.1 Top artists who began their careers in a group in the 1960s and went solo

Artist	Began solo	Last chart year	Length of chart career	Number of charting songs	Number of top 10 songs
Cher	1965	2002	38	33	10
Carlos Santana	1969	2005	37	24	6
Paul McCartney	1971	2005	35	46	17
George Harrison	1970	2002	33	17	5
Kenny Rogers	1976	2006	31	32	9
Darlene Love	1963	1993	31	4	0
Dion	1960	1989	30	24	8
Eric Clapton	1970	1998	29	27	6
Paul Simon	1962	1990	29	21	6
Ben E. King	1960	1986	27	22	4
Neil Sedaka	1958	1980	23	30	9
David Crosby	1971	1993	23	6	0
Glen Campbell	1961	1981	21	36	5
John Lennon	1969	1988	20	18	7
Jerry Butler	1958	1977	20	39	3
Bill Medley	1968	1987	20	6	1
Smokey Robinson	1973	1991	19	25	4
Diana Ross	1970	1986	17	41	11
David Ruffin	1969	1985	17	8	2
Mick Jagger	1978	1993	16	8	1
Graham Nash	1971	1986	16	8	0
Frankie Valli	1966	1980	15	14	4
Eddie Kendricks	1971	1985	15	15	2
John Fogerty	1972	1986	15	9	1
Stephen Stills	1970	1984	15	10	0
Neil Young	1970	1983	14	11	1
Roger Daltrey	1973	1985	13	8	0
Ringo Starr	1970	1981	12	14	7
Peter Cetera	1986	1997	12	13	5
John Stewart	1969	1979	11	4	1

Source: Whitburn 2007 [153]

Of the 232 groups that charted in the 1960s, over a quarter were listed on Pollstar.com as performing live in 2009. The group still performing live with the greatest longevity was Frankie Valli and the Four Seasons. The vocal group first charted in 1956 and was originally composed of Valli, his two brothers, and one other friend. Other than Valli, the lead singer, none of the other original members still perform with the group. The Four Seasons were very much a 1950s-model group. They were vocalists who were backed by studio musicians and most of their hit songs were written by professional songwriters who were not members of the group. This is also true of two groups that first charted in 1964: The Temptations and The Four Tops, who are still touring today each with only one original member.

Groups from the 1960s who are still performing today include the Animals, Box Tops, Cowsills, Deep Purple, The Fireballs, Manfred Mann, Rascals, Turtles, and

Vanilla Fudge though mostly without all of the original members. Though the lead singer died in 1970, Robbie Krieger and Ray Manzarek continue to tour as 50% of The Doors. Though these are only a few examples, they do provide support for the Chuck Tharp Hypothesis that the songs were more important than the groups. The question is can these groups continue to tour once all of the original members are deceased as have groups from the 1950s such as The Coasters and The Platters?

The groups of the 1960s represented a major break with groups in the Big Band era. There were fewer members, they had less musical knowledge than their predecessors, but the survival rates of the groups compare favorably with other industries. The four to five member rock band remained the model for group organization through the 1960s and 1970s, but by 1980 there was a new kind of music and a new organization of the group. This genre of music was known as rap or hip-hop music. It represents as radical a break with the 1960s model as the latter did with the Big Bands.

1.6 The Hip-hop Group

Baby boomers who are sometimes "stranded in the sixties" generally have a low opinion of rap/hip-hop music. This is ironic because the rap/hip-hop artists have accomplished a revolution in the music industry that parallels and, in some respects, exceeds the accomplishments of the artists of the 1950s and 1960s. Like the early rock bands, rap/hip-hop artists were viewed as having less musical ability. Certainly this was the case since they did not play the instruments used in a typical rock and roll band. However, was rock and roll any less musical because the bands didn't read sheet music? It seems that one way changes in musical style are delineated is that those performing the new musical style are considered to be less accomplished musicians.

This was certainly how early rock and roll was viewed by trained musicians, and it was certainly the case with the rise of "punk rock" in the late 1970s and 1980s. Bands like the Sex Pistols and the Ramones turned that lack of musicianship into a style that was distinctly different from that prevailing in the disco-era of the late 1970s. Johnny Ramone never picked an instrumental interlude in any Ramones' song, opting to play barred chords instead. However, the structure of the punk rock band reverted back to the Buddy Holly and the Crickets' model: lead guitar, rhythm guitar, bass, and drums. Other genres, especially rhythm and blues groups, added horn sections and there was some resurgence of vocal groups such as The Commodores in the 1970s. There was no radical break with the rock band organization until rap and hip-hop emerged in the early 1980s.

Just as the rock bands reduced the size of the group from 30 or more hired musicians to four or five in the group, the early rap groups were composed of one or two rappers using microphones and a DJ using a turntable, all electronically amplified. The turntable itself became a musical instrument through the development of "scratching"—or manipulating the needle over the record to alter the recorded sound. DJs who used two turntables to mix the sounds were among the first to create new music by "sampling"—taking a portion of one song and using it in a new composition. Rap/hip-hop artists not only drew upon the music of the past, especially of the 1950s and 1960s, they used an old technology in a new way and were among the first to use digital sampling.

One of the first rap records was "Rapper's Delight" by a group composed of three males from Harlem called the Sugarhill Gang. The song reached number 36 on the *Billboard* Hot 100 Singles chart in 1980 after reaching number 4 on the *Billboard* R&B charts in 1979. The most successful early group, however, was undoubtedly Run-D.M.C. who were elected to the Rock and Roll Hall of Fame in 2008. Their breakout hit in 1986 was "Walk This Way" which was a 1977 hit for Aerosmith. In the Run-D.M.C. version, two members of Aerosmith, Steve Tyler and Joe Perry, performed on the remake.

Like the early rock groups, the rap/hip-hop artists were signed to independent recording companies and not the Majors. However, the rap artists differed significantly from the typical rock group in that they developed a financially successful business model. Songwriters in the 1950s and 1960s often lost one-half of their royalties to a music publishing company owned by someone else. Rap/hip-hop artists created their own publishing companies. Rather than pay a producer a percentage of record sales, rap/hip-hop artists either became their own producers or used the Norman Petty model and put producers on as co-writers. Though musicians since the 1950s had been in movies, and the rap/hip-hop artists continued this tradition, they also expanded into non-entertainment industries such as clothing and other consumer items. Many of the successful solo rap/hip-hop artists were also first in a group (see Table 1.2).

Though it may be too early to determine survival rates on the *Billboard* Rap/Hip-hop charts in this genre, it appears that rap/hip-hop groups may have shorter charting careers when compared with groups in the 1960s. Where the most successful groups from the 1960s had careers of around 15 years, the top groups in the rap/hip-hop genre have careers of about 9 years. However, Run-D.M.C. charted from 1983 to 2000—18 years. This is the same as the average charting career for 1960s groups that are also in the Rock and Roll Hall of Fame. No other rap/hip-hop group has charted this long, but this does not rule out the possibility that some may have careers of 20 years or more. Can rap/hip-hop groups sustain music careers of 30–40 years? Can these groups continue on for 50 years or more as have The Coasters and The Platters after all of the original members are deceased? To the extent the Chuck Tharp Hypothesis is correct and the focus is more on the artist and their performance of a song, the less likely that people will want to hear someone else perform Run-D.M.C. songs. Though one suspects that the longevity of the songs is shorter than those of the early rock period, as noted, a counter to this is financial success and this success is often based on the fact that many rap/hip-hop artists are really serial entrepreneurs who expand their activities into other entertainment outlets or in clothing, and so on [113, 128].

Table 1.2 Rap/hip-hop artists, talents and group membership

Artist	Talents	Group
2Pac	Rapper, actor	Digital underground, thug life
50 Cent	Rapper, songwriter	G-unit
Aaliyah	Singer, actress	
Alicia Keys	Singer, songwriter, keyboardist	
Ashanti	Singer, songwriter	The Inc.
Babyface	Singer, songwriter, producer, multi-instrumentalist	Manchild, the Deele
Bobby Brown		New edition
Busta Rhymes	Rapper, songwriter, actor	Leaders of the new school
Dr. Dre	Rapper, producer, actor	N.W.A. World Class Wreckin' Cru
Eminem	Rapper, actor	D12
Faith Evans	Singer, actor	
Ginuwine	Singer, songwriter	Physical wonder
Ice Cube	Rapper, actor, songwriter	N.W.A. Westside Connection, one million strong
Ja Rule	Rapper, actor	The Inc.
Jay-Z	Rapper, songwriter, record label founder	Frequent guest rapper
Joe	Singer, songwriter, guitarist	
LL Cool J	Rapper, songwriter, actor	
Ludacris	Rapper, songwriter, actor	Disturbing the peace
Mariah Carey	Singer, songwriter, producer, actor	
Mary J. Blige	Singer, songwriter, actor	
Missy Elliott	Rapper, songwriter, producer	Sista
Monica	Singer	
Nas	Rapper, songwriter, actor	The firm, QB finest
Nelly	Rapper	St. Lunatics
Puff Daddy/P. Diddy	Rapper, songwriter, actor, entrepreneur	Rev Run and The Christmas All Stars
R. Kelly	Singer, songwriter, producer, multi-instrumentalist	
Snoop Dogg	Rapper, songwriter, actor	213, Rev Run and The Christmas All Stars
The Notorious B.I.G.	Rapper, songwriter	
Usher	Singer, songwriter, actor	

Source: Whitburn 2007 [153]

Has rap/hip-hop produced a group comparable to The Beatles? No, but no genre or era has done so either. It is highly unlikely that anyone will ever come close to the artistic and financial success and the impact on society equal to that of The Beatles. However, has the rap/hip-hop genre produced music as good as The Animals, Herman's Hermits, or The Box Tops? Baby boomers may think not, but they are probably wrong.

Chapter 2
Hitsville: Writing a Hit Song

Making a living from composing music has never been easy. F. M. Scherer [124] has painstakingly made estimates of the income of the classical composers in the eighteenth and nineteenth centuries. Mozart was not wealthy and wrote a voluminous amount of music. Scherer found, for the evidence available for 23 composers, that the top two accounted for 44% of the wealth of all of the composers in the group. Franz Schubert and Mozart died in debt. In fact, when compared with other art forms like painting or sculpture, composers earned far less. In the early 1700s, under the influence of the Lutheran religion, musicians attained a higher status and influence in Germany than elsewhere in the world at the time ([39], p. 133). By the late eighteenth century, they were able to attain a steady income from compositions and performances ([39], p. 138). Most well-known composers of the period distributed their work through sheet music which provided a considerable portion of their total income ([39], p. 140).

The economics of songwriting are quite interesting because they differ from that of most markets for goods and services. Songwriting is really a market for ideas—intellectual property. We are all familiar with tangible, physical goods whose supply is limited because real physical resources are required in their production. But what is required for songwriting? Certainly a basic language skill and musical ability, but beyond this, virtually anyone can potentially be a songwriter. Perhaps the most fundamental change in creating music that has occurred over the Rock and Roll Era is that no longer is there a specialization in composing music or writing lyrics. Evidence of this is that more artists "do it all" when it comes to creating music: compose the music, write lyrics, produce the recording, and so on. This also means that the number of artists credited with writing a particular song has also risen. Consider the case of Kelly Clarkson who won the first season of *American Idol* in 2002. Her debut album went double platinum and her second album went six times platinum. However, she was forced to cancel her original tour in support of her third album. Instead of large venues and a summer-long tour, she had a shortened fall tour. What was the problem? Her previous smash album *Breakaway* contained songs she co-wrote with experienced songwriters. Kelly decided that she wanted to write most of the songs on the album *My December*. Clark's decline in sales led Clive Davis, one of the most successful producers and promoters in the industry, to comment that

R.J. Phillips, *Rock and Roll Fantasy?: The Reality of Going from Garage Band to Superstardom*, SpringerBriefs in Business 35, DOI 10.1007/978-1-4614-5900-2_2,

singers shouldn't try to be songwriters. Davis' argument is that to be really good at something requires your full attention and effort. You can't be expected to be the best at two things. A lot of musicians are actors, but how many are in the Rock and Roll Hall of Fame who also won Academy Awards? Cher is the only name that comes to mind.

In a blog, John Cougar Mellankamp [102] expressed the dilemma of the artist who tries to do everything:

> These days, some people suggest that it is up to the artist to create avenues to sell the music of his own creation. In today's environment, is it realistic to expect someone to be a songwriter, recording artist, record company and the P.T. Barnum, so to speak, of his own career? Of course not.

Has this change in the creation of music resulted in a decrease in productivity—more songwriters needed to create a number one hit? The implications of the decline of specialization is the focus of this chapter. This chapter reviews the history of songwriting in the USA from colonial times with a focus on the production process, i.e., the putting together of music and lyrics to create a song. The most important factors in this evolution are changes in technology and the structure of compensation for composers.

2.1 The Rise of the Popular Song in the USA

The earliest songs that are considered American popular music were all songs where words were added to existing melodies. If you could presume the tunes were well known, creating new words made the song accessible to a wider group. According to Isaac Goldberg, the first popular song in the American Colonies was the "Liberty Song" which was published in the *Boston Gazette* on July 18, 1768 ([68], p. 17). The words were written by John Dickinson of Delaware and inspired by the Massachusetts Legislature's effort to rescind the imposition of duties and taxes by England. Though the lyrics were original, the music was taken from a song written in England in 1759 ([68], p. 18). One of the oldest "American" songs still known today is "Yankee Doodle" [6]. This song was written by a British army surgeon Richard Shuckburgh in September 1755 at Fort Crailo, NY, set to the "Doodle-doo" song from "The Beggar's Opera" by John Gay composed in 1728. The song was sung by the British troops during the Revolutionary War with new lyrics to ridicule Colonial leaders such as John Hancock. The American militia began to play the song and added anti-British lyrics:

> Yankee Doodle is the tune,
> That we all delight in;
> It suits for feasts, it suits for fun,
> And just as well for fighting!

This established a connection between war and popular music that would continue in US history. The "Star-Spangled Banner" which Francis Scott Key wrote as a poem during the War of 1812, was put to the familiar tune of a British drinking song of the Anacreonic Society, a drinking club based in a pub in the Strand, London [74].

The production process of popular music was thus established: the tune is created first, and then lyrics are written to fit the tune. As Goldberg notes, this was precisely the method of production used later in Tin Pan Alley—write the music, then the lyrics ([68], p. 19).

When did the first American tunes appear? Though the music of the northern states was dominated by religious music from England, the southern states imported their music under quite different arrangements: slavery. It is no exaggeration to say that the music we think of as "American" music had its origins in the melodies sung by slaves in the southern states. However, the story is not one of African–American songwriters given credit for their songs, rather, white composers took the tunes, wrote lyrics, and popularized the songs. The mode of performance of the original American music was the minstrel show. Though not the originator of minstrel shows, Stephan F. Foster is the most recognized American composer who wrote his tunes in the mid-nineteenth century for minstrel shows where whites, often in blackface, sang his songs. The list of songs he wrote would be familiar to most Americans today: "Swanee River," "De Camptown Races," "My Old Kentucky Home," among others. These songs were all written for minstrel shows. Though the state of Kentucky adopted "My Old Kentucky Home" as the state song, the lyrics were changed to omit what we would now view as lyrics offensive to African–Americans.

There was not much protection for songwriters in the nineteenth century in the USA, but it was not a totally *laissez faire* system. In Article I, Section 8 of the US Constitution copyright is given "To promote the progress of science and useful arts, by securing for limited times to authors and inventors the exclusive right to their respective writings and discoveries." The Copyright Act of 1790 focused on books, charts, and maps. At the time, the primary means of accessing music compositions was through sheet music.

In the period prior to recorded sound, a songwriter or songwriters composed the music, wrote the lyrics, and then split the royalties on sheet music sales with a music publisher. "Jobbers" or "pluggers" were employed by the music publishing companies to persuade singers to perform their songs. The possibility of recorded song, which began with the player piano, continued with the rise of the phonograph. Radio in the 1920s was also to play an important role, though it was reported in a *New York Times* article of May 29, 1908 that the music instrument producers argued at the time that the such technological advances as radio were a means to increase sheet music sales [139].

2.2 Tin Pan Alley

Though there was American music from colonial days, it is with the beginning of Tin Pan Alley in the 1890s that we see the rise of modern popular music as we know it in the USA today. Prior to recorded sound, people had musical instruments at home. The piano was quite popular, but there were other instruments such as guitars. Some towns even had bands composed of local citizens. The way composers profited from their songs was primarily through the sale of sheet music. The establishment of Tin Pan Alley in Manhattan was driven by the desire of songwriters to sell their output

Table 2.1 Top pop music songwriters, 1945

Writer	Titles	Specialization
Sammy Cahn	23	Lyrics
Johnny Mercer	21	Performer, lyrics
Jule Styne	19	Music
Oscar Hammerstein	11	Lyrics
Richard Rodgers	11	Music
Harold Arlen	11	Music
Jimmy Van Heusen	10	Music
Irving Berlin	9	Lyrics/music
Johnny Burke	9	Lyrics
Harry Warren	8	Music/lyrics
Moe Jaffe	7	Music/lyrics/bandleader
Sunny Skylar	6	Performer, composer, lyricist, publisher

Source: Whitburn 2002 [150]

to the public for profit. One of the popular music pioneers and Tin Pan Alley founders was Charles K. Harris who began his songwriting career by opening an office in Milwaukee, Wisconsin with the sign outside his door reading: "Songs written to order" ([68], p. 92). A lyricist added words to music created by a composer, and thus two individuals were involved in the writing of a song. Table 2.1 shows the top songwriters for 1945 who typically wrote for Broadway shows and were very much in the Tin Pan Alley mold. For the most part, they were songwriters who specialized in either writing lyrics or composing music and were not producers or performers. The only exception was Johnny Mercer who was both a performer and a songwriter while Sunny Skylar was a performer, composer, lyricist, and publisher.

Producing sheet music required someone to score the song and then have it printed up. This was the function of music publishing companies. The songwriter could sell all rights to the song to the publishing company for a fixed fee or else the songwriter and the publishing company could make arrangements to share the revenue from selling the sheet music. These revenues were called royalties. Three of Foster's most popular songs, including "My Old Kentucky Home," were sold for $50 ([68], p. 45). Selling the song for a fixed price may not be a good economic decision in a world with an elaborate copyright protection scheme, but it probably makes some sense in the nineteenth century because of the costs involved in trying to collect further payments from anyone who might produce sheet music of his songs or perform them live. It is also likely that Foster sold his song for much less than what he could have earned if he had been able to collect royalties on his composition. The institutional structure of the music industry was undeveloped and there were clearly problems in the market for songwriting.

Though the split between songwriter and music publisher could potentially be whatever the two parties agreed to, a "rule of thumb" rate was to have a fifty–fifty split of royalties and this rate became institutionalized [106]. Was this a *fair* split? If you were a new and unknown songwriter, 50% might be pretty good. However, if you had written a few hit songs, you could probably negotiate a better split. With the passage of the Copyright Act of 1909, composers could earn royalties from the sale of records in addition to the sale of sheet music.

Prior to the digital and Internet revolution, the focus on making it in rock and roll music was to earn royalties on the sale of recorded music. This royalty income largely replaced the royalty income from sheet music, which had been the main source of income. For most of the era of recorded music the compensation for those involved in music production was well established. Songwriters and music publishers received performance royalties—these are paid whenever a composition is performed in public and mechanical royalties went to artists and labels based on records sold—whether these were vinyl records, reel-to-reel tapes, cassette tapes, or compact disks (CDs).

In the typical contract, mechanical royalties were split among band members after the costs of recording and touring were deducted. Since each song used on an album must be licensed and performance royalties paid the music publishing company distributed the funds to the songwriter. Radio paid performance royalties to the song writer and publishing company but not to the artists and record companies. Performance royalties were also paid whenever the song was performed in public.

The process of producing a song for a record involved a division of labor. Songwriters wrote for singers and a producer was in charge of recording. Everyone had their assigned tasks and the reward structure was set in place. The royalty payment to the music company was intended to cover their costs in promoting the song and they employed song "pluggers" to perform this function. Songwriters were generally not singers. The singers came into the studio, performed the music under a billed-by-the-hour time constraint. Producers got a royalty cut on the records or a flat fee for operating the recording equipment.

The model for songwriting production in the 1950s and 1960s was, like the Tin Pan Alley model, one of songwriting teams—usually two or three people. For example, in the 1950s there was the songwriting team Jerry Lieber and Mike Stoller, and in the 1960s there was John Lennon and Paul McCartney. Producers were occasionally also songwriters or owned music publishing companies, but more typical was the case of George Martin who was not given songwriting credits on The Beatles' songs, nor did he own The Beatles' music publishing company. However, as can be seen in Table 2.2, songwriters by 1965 were frequently also performers. The Beatles and Bob Dylan are prominent examples, though songwriting teams, such as Holland-Dozier-Holland (HDH) who wrote songs for The Supremes and others, were still important.

What introduced changes to this compensation structure was the cost of reproducing a recording fell—close to zero with the MP3 format—and also distribution costs fell with the expansion of the Internet globally. While the songwriters and publishing companies continued to flourish, the artists and labels saw their revenue decline dramatically with the rise of Napster and illegal downloading of MP3 files.

Table 2.2 Top pop music songwriters, 1965

Writer	Titles	Comments
Eddie Holland	13	Writing team HDH
Lamont Dozier	11	Writing team HDH
Brian Holland	11	Writing team HDH
Smokey Robinson	13	Performer
Warren Moore	9	Songwriting team
Bob Dylan	9	Performer
John Lennon	10	Writing Team L/M, performer
Paul McCartney	10	Writing Team L/M, performer
Roger Miller	7	Performer
Sonny Bono	7	Performer
Curtis Mayfield	12	Performer
Wes Farrell	8	Lyrics/music
Tony Hatch	7	Lyrics/music

Source: Whitburn 2006b [152]

2.3 Songwriters in the Digital Age

How have songwriters adapted in the Digital Age? Increasingly artists are vertically integrated firms, i.e., they are involved at every stage of music production from songwriting to producing to distributing. For those who think of popular songwriting teams such as Richard Rodgers and Oscar Hammerstein II, or John Lennon and Paul McCartney, it may seem puzzling to learn that in recent years the average number of co-writers for a popular song has increased significantly beyond two (see Fig. 2.1). As an example, Mariah Carey's *Billboard* top single of 2005 "We Belong Together" lists ten co-writers. Why does it now take ten people to achieve a number one song when it took one or two people in the past? This would appear to be a decline in productivity of songwriters. A corollary of this change is that increasingly songwriters do not specialize in songwriting but are also frequently performers and producers (see Table 2.1). In the case of "We Belong Together," the large number of songwriters is a result of both the use of sampling or interpolating (use of parts of previously recorded songs) and giving the producer songwriting credits.

Consider the Top 10 songwriters for 2005 in Table 2.3. Songwriters today can be compared with songwriters in the Tin Pan Alley era (Table 2.1), who, as noted, were mostly specialized in writing either lyrics or music and with the singer/songwriters of the 1960s (Table 2.2). Whereas previously the producer's income typically depended upon physical sales of records, today it depends upon the performance royalties of the copyrighted songs. This is important because songwriters have always received performance income, but producers have not. Primarily rap and hip-hop artists have brought about this change due to the digital revolution and music genre innovation (Fig. 2.1).

Is the use of nine co-writers by Mariah Carey evidence of a decline in the productivity of songwriters since it takes more songwriters to create a number one hit today than in the past? After all, it only took two people to write "I Want to Hold

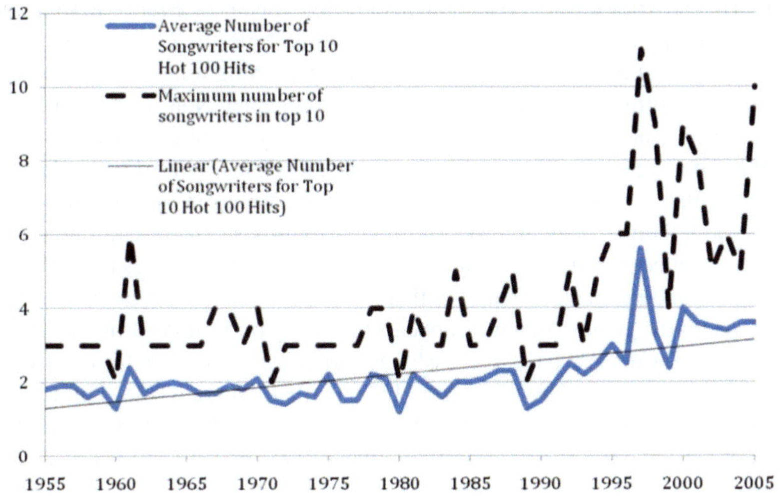

Fig. 2.1 Average number of songwriters for top 10 hot 100 hits, 1955–2005. *Source*: Whitburn 2006a [151]

Table 2.3 Top songwriters on the *Billboard* hot 100, 2005

Songwriter	Number of titles	Performer	Producer
Curtis J. Jackson, Jr. (50 Cent)	13	X	
Jermaine Dupri	8	X	X
Christopher Bridges (Ludacris)	6	X	
Scott Storch	7		X
Kanye West	9	X	X
Johnta Austin	5		X
Sean Garrett	6	X	X
Andre Young (Dr. Dre)	7	X	X
Mike Elizondo	6	X	X
Mark Batson	5		X
Mariah Carey	4	X	X
Jonathan H. "Lil Jon" Smith	6	X	X

Source: Whitburn 2006b [152]

Your Hand," the number one song of 1964 for The Beatles. A decline in productivity would be the explanation if no innovations had occurred since 1964. However, the increase in the number of co-writers on songs is driven by the innovation of sampling and impacted by the current structure of compensation in the music industry (mechanical royalties are declining while performance royalties are rising due to ringtones and so on).

In the Tin Pan Alley music production model, there was specialization in songwriting. Sammy Cahn, the top songwriter of 1945, wrote the lyrics to 23 top songs. Richard Rodgers and Oscar Hammerstein together wrote 11 charting songs in the same year. In 1965, the songwriting team of HDH charted 11 hits together. None of these individuals were performing artists. Each specialized in writing lyrics or composing music. By 2005, the top songwriter Curtis L. Jackson, Jr. (50 Cent) wrote 13 charting songs, and he was also a performer. Eight of the nine remaining in the top ten were also producers and their average number of hit songs was six. The remaining artist who was not a producer was Ludacris, and he wrote six chartings songs as well.

Though economists since Adam Smith have thought that specialization and division of labor creates the greatest output, it appears that today performing artists can be songwriters and producers and be as successful as earlier songwriters in terms of charting hits. One change noted by Galenson [61] is that whereas the Tin Pan Alley songwriters wrote their best songs when they were in their thirties and forties, songwriters in the early rock period wrote their best songs when they were in their twenties, and this still appears true today.

2.4 Cover Songs

The emphasis early on in the recording industry was to focus on the "hit" record. In 1900, the top ten songs included two versions each by different artists of four songs. From Tin Pan Alley days to the early days of rock and roll, it was quite common for other artists to cover a hit song. Thus, Johnny Mercer might have a hit song and then Bing Crosby, Tommy Dorsey, or Judy Garland and others would cover it. The industry was dominated by "cover songs"—different versions of a song someone else had already recorded. It was obviously in the interest of the composer and the music publishing companies to sell as many records as possible, and this meant having as many artists and labels record and sell the song as possible. In the period from the beginning of recorded sound until the Rock and Roll Era in the 1950s, this is typically how the recording industry operated. The motivation for releasing cover versions through the first half of the twentieth century was clearly for more record companies and artists to earn income from a song that had been demonstrated to have popular appeal.

Does covering a song imply that it is better than other songs? Probably, if there are many cover versions. For example, in 1900, the number one song was "When You Were Sweet Sixteen" recorded by George J. Gaskin, a popular Irish tenor, on the Columbia label. It was on the charts for 10 weeks and peaked in November and remained number one for 8 weeks. This was a cover version because Jere Mahoney had released his version on Edison Records earlier in the year and it went to number one in April and remained number one for 5 weeks. The number two song of 1900, "Ma Tiger Lily" by Arthur Collins on Berliner Records was also a cover version of Jere Mahoney's version. Collins' version hit number one in September and remained number one for 6 weeks, while Mahoney's version on Edison had been number one for 5 weeks in July. The number three song, "A Bird in a Gilded Cage" by Steve Porter on Columbia was number one in June for 6 weeks and then covered by Harry MacDonough on Edison Records whose version peaked at number two in October for 3 weeks. Though this pattern of established artists doing cover versions continued throughout the early decades of the twentieth century, it became less likely that cover versions of number one songs would also be number one. However, in 1947 "Peg O" My Heart' was a number one song for both The Harmonicats and Buddy Clark. In the same year, "Open the Door, Richard" was a number one for The Three Flames and Count Basie [149].

In 1955, a year which is a transition year to the Rock and Roll Era, three different versions of "The Ballad of David Crockett" made the *Billboard* charts. It was a number one hit for Bill Hayes for 5 weeks beginning in March, a number five hit for "Tennessee" Ernie Ford for 4 weeks beginning in May, and also a number five for 4 weeks beginning in May for Fess Parker, who played Davy Crockett in the Disney television show.

Though covering popular songs resulted in a very profitable industry, especially for songwriters and music publishing companies, it also meant that fewer new songs were introduced. The industry could be characterized as one that valued a steady income stream to songwriters and publishers and there was less innovation in popular music. Given the introduction of the lower cost recording studio in the post-World War II period, it could have been just an opportunity for independent record companies to do cheaper cover versions of the major recording companies' hits. What upset this structure was the rise of rock and roll, especially beginning with Elvis Presley and others in 1956. Presley was clearly the first artist to be different and innovative enough so that no one covered his songs in the same year. Presley's first charting song was "Heartbreak Hotel" in 1956.

Rock and roll was heavily influenced by the black artists in the rhythm and blues genre and one of Presley's best known songs "Hound Dog" was a cover of Big Mama Thornton's original version. Though few would give him the credit, Pat Boone played an important role in the rock and roll revolution. Boone's first charting song was "Two Hearts," a song that went to number eight on the R&B charts for The Charms in 1955. On May 14, 1955, Fats Domino debuted "Ain't that a Shame" on the R&B charts, and it went to number one and stayed on the charts for 26 weeks. On July 9, 1955, Pat Boone released his version of "Ain't that a Shame," and it became his first number one song and remained on the charts for 20 weeks. Boone's releases from 1955 to 1958 were mostly covers, many of them of songs originally by black artists, but he also covered Glenn Miller and Frank Sinatra, among others. Boone's career was one characterized as almost always doing cover songs—some going back to the early part of the twentieth century. In 1997, Boone released his first album in many years, and it contained covers of heavy metal songs. Pat Boone was not a songwriter, he was a singer.

Though some accused Boone and his record company, Dot, of "ripping off" black artists, in fact what Boone's cover versions did was bring black artists recognition to teenagers, and especially white teenagers. Thus the function of cover songs in the early years of rock and roll were to expand the opportunities for the original artists and ultimately helped artists like Little Richard achieve great success on the charts.

2.5 The Beatles Change the Cover Song Game

Boone and Presley were by no means the only artists in the Rock and Roll Era to use cover songs. Though The Beatles were unusual in the early 1960s in writing most of their songs, they too did cover versions when they recorded their first albums. The Beatles covered not only black artists, but also early singer/songwriters such as Buddy Holly. However, something different happens when it came to covers of The Beatles' songs. The Beatles' "Hey Jude" was covered more times than any other *Billboard* number one song from 1946 to 2008. It has been covered 58 times, while Simon and Garfunkel's "Bridge over Troubled Waters" has been covered 42 times. The number three most covered was The Beatles song "I Want to Hold Your Hand," which was the number one *Billboard* song for 1964, was covered 24 times that year and at least 16 more times since then. Elvis Presley's "Heartbreak Hotel" has been covered 29 times and ranks fourth.

This is reminiscent of what happened in the Tin Pan Alley days, but what is different beginning with The Beatles is that there are many more cover versions, but few of them make the charts. Only two cover versions of "Hey Jude" made the charts at number 23 (Wilson Pickett) and number 119 by Paul Mauriat, both in the year following the release of The Beatles' original in 1968. Only one cover version of "I Want to Hold Your Hand" charted and that was the Boston Pops Orchestra with Arthur Fielder conducting and peaking at number 55. There is no doubt that this splurge of cover versions of The Beatles was an attempt to appropriate profits for other artists and labels, as it also enriched Lennon/McCartney and their publishing company.

The Beatles represent the start of a new approach to music—one where artists and labels would take greater risk in order to try to replicate the phenomenal success of The Beatles. This is why 1964 is such a landmark year. Henceforth, instead of focusing on stability of income and familiarity with tunes, the emphasis would be on finding something new, and that often meant finding a new artist.

But how do you replicate the success of The Beatles? One could argue that John, Paul, George and Ringo as Beatle phenomena had some characteristics of a "Black Swan Event"—a huge unexpected band with an enormous impact but one that has not really been explained to date. No one in any era can compare to the artistic and commercial accomplishments of The Beatles. It resulted in an even greater emphasis on the hit song and consequently led to recording companies investing more in finding new superstars.

Though popular artists continue to do cover versions, the fact that in general they did not do better than the original indicates that with the arrival of The Beatles the focus shifts from the uniqueness of the songs to the uniqueness of the artist. There are, of course, exceptions such as Whitney Houston's 1992 version of "I Will Always Love You" which went to number one. Dolly Parton's original was released in 1974 but did not make the top 100 and charted again in 1982 at number 53. Houston's version was featured in a movie and Houston was at the peak of her popularity on the pop charts in the early 1990s. But covers can also involve innovation. An example would be Jimi Hendrix's version of Dylan's "All Along the Watchtower."

2.6 Cover Songs in the Digital Age: Sampling and Interpolating

Covering songs by other artists has a long tradition in the music industry and it continues to the present, but with interesting innovations. I discovered an interesting example of this innovation while perusing the *Billboard* Hot 100 one week in the spring of 2010. I came upon a song that intrigued me because of the list of co-writers for the song. The title of the song was "Lemonade" and the artist was Gucci Mane, a rap artist whose real name was Radric Davis. I didn't know much about him, except that he was currently in jail. Listed as co-writers of the song were S. Crawford, his producer and two other names that someone who learned to play the guitar in the mid-1960s would likely recognize: J. H. Kaylan and M. Volman. The latter two co-writers were none other than Howard Kaylan and Mark Volman who were the lead singers for The Turtles in the 1960s and who later joined Frank Zappa's Mothers of Invention under the pseudonyms of Flo and Eddie. The Turtles doing rap music? How could this be? It turns out that Mane had taken the melody from a Flo and Eddie song written in the 1970s, "Keep it Warm" and used it for his chorus. What was even more amusing were the lyrics to the Flo and Eddie song. Where Mane sang "Lemon in the shade with my feet up," Flo and Eddie's lyrics were "Money in the bank to keep us warm." The first verse of the Flo and Eddie song was about the need to write songs that would generate royalties over time. It looks like they succeeded.

The use of sampling or interpolating is quite common in current songwriting in all genres, though it originated with rap music. What does this say about contemporary songwriting? Is Mane less of a songwriter because he "ripped off" Flo and Eddie? Or is his use of an obscure song a creative innovation in songwriting? The fact is, Mane had a charting song and Flo and Eddie earned royalties. Is very unlikely that anyone would be unhappy with this situation. Of course, had Mane not given credit to Flo and Eddie, it would be quite a different story.

Contemporary popular music has always used an element of older musical styles, regardless of the time period. In the early days of Tin Pan Alley, popular songs were sung by different artists. The innovation was in the interpretation of the song given by different artists. Many of the early rock and roll songs were new versions of older rhythm and blues songs. Though The Beatles were undoubtedly the most unique songwriters, even Lennon and McCartney were influenced by earlier styles and the fact that their producer, George Martin, was able to bring to their recordings his experience with recording other genres of music. If one listens to "For the Benefit of Mr. Kite" or "When I'm Sixty-four" from *Sgt. Pepper's* the influence of earlier musical styles can be clearly heard. Lennon's "In My Life" is distinctive for its use of the harpsichord, an instrument that would have been found in music written by Mozart.

Innovation is about creating something new from something old. Not only is this found in songwriting, but this is in fact a defining characteristic of musical eras. The future always builds on the past. It was true in Bing Crosby's era in the early twentieth century, and it is true today for the Black Eyed Peas or any other group in popular music. It definitely does not mean that the music of Gucci Mane in and of itself is any less "real" music than that of Frank Sinatra. Innovation in music style will be explored further in the next chapter.

Chapter 3
Innovation: Will You Ever Hear Surf Music Again?

As we have seen, musicians are creative in putting a band together and in songwriting; however, to be successful, they must create a sound that is distinctive. Musical styles are differentiated on the basis of elements of sound such as rhythm, melody, harmony, and tone. Though musicians must have their own style, most compose within a particular genre of musical style such as jazz, country and western, rock, hip-hop, and so on. We can also compare the musical styles in different eras. The Tin Pan Alley songs, mostly written for Broadway, were quite different from the rock and roll songs of the 1950s which were simpler in both musical structure and lyrics. Fewer humans and a greater reliance on electrical amplification or electronic reproduction of sound characterized the Rock and Roll Era and rap music continued this trend.

Change in musical style requires the creation of something new. When analyzing the dynamics of change in an industry, economists typically talk about inventions and innovations. Invention is the creation of a new technology—the phonograph which Thomas Edison patented in 1877 would be a good example. An invention that is successfully brought to the market is what we call an innovation. Lots of things are invented, but it is only when they can be utilized in the economy to produce something that is new or at a lower cost is it considered an innovation. Edison thought that his dictation machine would primarily be useful for the busy executive, and only after others improved on his original design and began to market the phonograph for entertainment did Edison abandon its business use. These concepts are useful in analyzing the music industry. Anybody can write a song (invention), but the problem is to get someone to listen to it and buy it (innovation). As discussed in the previous chapter, cover songs are also a way to innovate in performance and create new music. Like Edison and the phonograph, Hendrix turned Dylan's acoustic invention of "All Along the Watchtower" into a landmark innovation with his amplified, electric, and psychedelic musical style.

Given the changing demographics and tastes of music consumers, the creativity of musicians, and the preponderance of technological change affecting the music industry, innovation in musical style is a fundamental characteristic of popular music. Though every recorded song that makes the charts is an innovation, some

R.J. Phillips, *Rock and Roll Fantasy?: The Reality of Going from Garage Band to Superstardom*, SpringerBriefs in Business 35, DOI 10.1007/978-1-4614-5900-2_3,

last longer than others before they are replaced by new songs. Both invention and innovation have the connotation of something new, but it is important to recognize that they are based on something old—something borrowed from the past. This is also true of invention and innovation in music. You can't have MP3 files without computers, and you can't have Jimi Hendrix without Muddy Waters and, some would say, you cannot have The Beatles without Buddy Holly. It also means that current songs frequently harken back to an earlier musical style. This occurs not only whenever new versions of old songs are recorded but also whenever songs are sampled. Each song is a combination of something new and something old in a ratio that varies over the decades. Pablo Picasso was reported to have once said that good artists borrow, but great artists steal. This is also true in music and points out the thin line between old and new whenever there is an innovation in musical style or composition.

Innovation in music creates a supply and demand problem. First, consumers, especially teenagers, are always looking for new music. I can remember when I was in high school and a friend who had just come back from southern California brought two albums for me to hear. The first was *Freak Out*! by The Mothers of Invention and the second was *The Fugs' First Album*. Songs like "Hungry Freaks, Daddy," "Who are the Brain Police?" and "Boobs a lot" were songs that made a lasting impression on my 15-year-old psyche. A year later, a friend who was already in college brought home an album from a great new artist who had just released his first album in the USA. I will never forget hearing the opening notes of "Purple Haze" by Jimi Hendrix that was played on the old family console stereo. It was unlike anything I had ever heard. In the song "Third Stone from the Sun," Hendrix asks: "Will you ever hear surf music again?" Hendrix's "psychedelic" music was in many ways the antithesis of the clean, trebly sound of surf music.

I always sought out music that was different, and I think a lot of my friends did as well. I do not think that the desire for something new and different among teenagers has changed much in the past 40 years. The trick was to find something different that no one else had heard, but that everyone would love. Baby boomers tend to think that this experience was unique in the 1960s, but it continues with the present generation of teenagers. There has always been a demand for innovation in music—something that sounds different from what you have been used to listening to.

It appears, however, that something different is in short supply. So at the same time consumers seek music that is new or innovative, it is also the case that artists who are very innovative often have difficulty making it commercially. They are too obscure, too unknown, and the channels of communication sometimes make it difficult to transmit information to other consumers. The Internet solves this problem in principle because there is so much music available, and services like Rhapsody, Pandora, and Slacker help consumers find music they may like by gathering information on consumer tastes. If the Internet had existed in the 1960s, I could have potentially found Jimi Hendrix, Frank Zappa, and The Fugs on my own.

The number and size of the firms in an industry can also impact innovation. Most industries are neither monopolies nor characterized by a large number of small firms. Instead, industries typically have a few large firms and many small firms, and this is true of the music industry. Although the first decades of the recorded music industry in the early twentieth century were characterized by the domination of a few large firms, by the 1950s, the recording industry was divided into major and independent companies: referred to respectively as the "Majors" and the "Indies." In the 1950s, the Majors in the USA were Decca, Mercury, RCA-Victor, Columbia, Capitol, MGM, and ABC-Paramount. There were numerous Indies including Atlantic, Chess, Veejay, Sun, Liberty, Warner Brothers, and United Artists. It is no surprise that the rise of rock and roll was due mainly to the role of the Indies, and not the Majors. As already mentioned in an earlier chapter, Decca first recorded both Buddy Holly and the Crickets in the USA and The Beatles in the UK but failed to develop either artist. It is sometimes argued that one reason for the British invasion in the 1960s was that monopoly elements in the music industry (including radio) inhibited the development of rock and roll in Britain [79]. Though The Beatles were successful in Britain and signed to EMI, their career skyrocketed when they came to the USA.

The payoff for very innovative artists who initially have a tough time breaking into the business can be large. The Beatles' records were first issued on obscure independent labels like Veejay, Swan, and Tollie in the USA before being released by Capitol Records. The success of The Beatles changed the music industry dramatically because their success resulted in both Indies and Majors taking greater risks with new artists.

3.1 What Promotes Innovation in Music?

Innovation in music depends upon the state of technology, the music that consumers like, and the creativity of musicians. These three factors interact in often complex ways. Given that innovation is an essential element in popular music, it can still be the case that there can be either more or less innovation. Economists generally believe that when there are lots of firms and lots of competition, innovation will be greater in the industry. This assumes that the industry can easily be entered by new firms. It can also be the case that an industry where the costs are very high for research and development may require very large scale production so only a large monopoly firm would likely be successful. At one time, the telecommunications industry was considered a "natural" monopoly, i.e., the only way to supply everyone with a phone profitably was to have only one phone company and have it regulated by a government agency. The airline industry was a heavily regulated "shared monopoly." The Civil Aeronautics Board approved where airlines flew and how much they could charge. Today most public utilities supplying electricity are still monopolies that are highly regulated.

In the music industry, the Majors had an established market and stable revenue and had a vested interest (to use Thorstein Veblen's term) in maintaining the status quo. In fact, as was the case with Mitch Miller of Columbia, there was often an active hostility toward rock and roll. This hostility was driven not only by a dislike of the youth music, but due to the fact that the demand for songs such as Miller's "The Yellow Rose of Texas" fell as the rebellious rock and roll music flourished in the 1950s.

The music business, as Burke notes, is one which exhibits strong elements of the static element of the way the industry is organized which involves monopoly, but at the same time, also exhibits many elements of entrepreneurship such as creativity, risk-taking, and Research and Development (R&D) intensity ([23], p. 321); [113]. Baker [9] notes several interesting aspects of the music industry as it developed prior to the Digital Age. First, although dominated by large producers, low recording costs and wide availability of production facilities meant that entrance into the industry was not prohibitive for small producers. Secondly, rather than focusing on the number of units sold, it is more appropriate to concentrate on the number of titles issued. Baker says that because there is a tendency for records to be sold at a standard price, this implies that the market is not one where supply and demand determine price, but rather what fluctuates is the number of titles ([9], p. 29). Given uncertain demand for any individual title, the solution is for the record company to diversify its title offerings. Because the industry faces uncertainty of demand for any particular record, the mix of titles is constantly changing ([9], p. 33). Baker shows that a modest degree of title diversification serves to eliminate most of the perceived risk from the firm's uncertainty about overall demand ([9], p. 33).

In Baker's model, this suggests that in periods of intense competition, lots of titles are released, but this can create a potentially chaotic competitive environment. One could reasonably expect that the response to this would be industry mergers and a reduction in the number of firms so that the firms can then stabilize their revenue streams by selling fewer titles. Viewed as an industry with monopoly power on the part of record companies, but with uncertain demand, then the companies would issue fewer titles to compensate for the costs of introducing new artists and the uncertainty of demand ([9], pp. 35, 45). With the uncertainty of demand facing an individual producer, a stable industry in terms of revenue is problematic, Baker argues.

The emergence and survival of small firms adds another interesting aspect to the industry. The number of independent record companies has been an important factor in innovation in the music industry. While there have been small companies that have grown in size over the past 40 years, more often than not, the small independent is acquired by a Major. The story of Sun Records, which first recorded Elvis Presley, illustrates the problem for Indies who discover artists who are destined for greatness. Sam Phillips, the owner of Sun, sold the rights to Elvis to RCA-Victor. What RCA was able to do with Elvis was to utilize its financial resources and distribution network to make Elvis a bonafide megastar. As Phillips recognized, he could not do as much for Elvis as RCA could do. Though some later questioned Phillips' decision, in the 1950s environment, Phillips made the business decision that he could use the money from RCA to find another star of Elvis' stature. Though he never did, Phillips did play an important role in the development of the "Memphis Sound."

Before the Internet and digital recordings, the economies of scale in the music industry lay in manufacturing, distribution, marketing, and financing which enabled the large companies to get the music output to the public quickly. This offered great advantage to the established companies when dealing with a creative artist. Burke notes that, as in the case of Sun and RCA in the Elvis Presley case noted above, the Majors had a competitive advantage over the Indies in signing creative artists ([23], pp. 323–324).

Prior to the Digital Age, it would appear that the industry might be fairly stagnant and characterized largely by monopoly if it were not for the fact that signing a record deal is more appealing to new artists than it is to established artists with demonstrated and continuing market power ([23], p. 324). If there were more competition in the record company market, there would presumably be greater benefits to the new artists. Whenever there are only a few firms in an industry, then the firms are able to pay less for new artists and this usually means higher profits for the Majors.

The sources of both innovation and instability in the music industry are songs and artists. Songs can be old or new, and artists can be established or debuting. Having established artists record songs that are familiar to the public would presumably be the lowest risk strategy. The riskiest strategy would be to have debuting artists performing songs that the public had never heard. In addition, changes in musical style have typically been accompanied by a change in technology. Given these characteristics of the recorded music industry, what might the evolution of the industry look like?

Suppose we begin with the assumption that the industry starts out with a few firms that are seeking to establish a steady revenue stream in a new industry. We would expect to see established artists singing well known songs. This is, in fact, the case during the early years of the twentieth century once the phonograph established itself as a means to commercialize recorded songs. Singers from Broadway and Vaudeville recorded songs that were popular on stage. There were numerous cover versions of a favorite tune. Assuming music preferences are well established, then the companies have a pretty stable revenue stream. This corresponds to Period I in Fig. 3.1. What upsets this state of affairs is either a change in the musical tastes of the public, innovation by musicians, or a change in technology. All three of these changes occurred with the rise of the Jazz Age, which was the first period where popular music changed dramatically [142, 144]. Rather than playing from music scores, jazz was premised on improvisation. With jazz you had new artists, but the innovation was in varying themes on music that's often already known. Jazz was an innovation in covering songs and therefore could be characterized by Period II in the Fig. 3.1. The emergence of radio as a means to disseminate music to a wider audience helped promote both jazz and the swing music of the big bands.

The rise of swing music beginning in the mid-1930s and continuing through World War II was the era of the Big Bands playing live and on the radio. Radio became popular and the connection with the recorded music industry was evidenced by the purchase of Victor Talking Records by the Radio Corporation of America (RCA). While some initially saw radio as a threat to recorded music, live music broadcasts became popular. Instead of decreasing the sales of recorded music, it

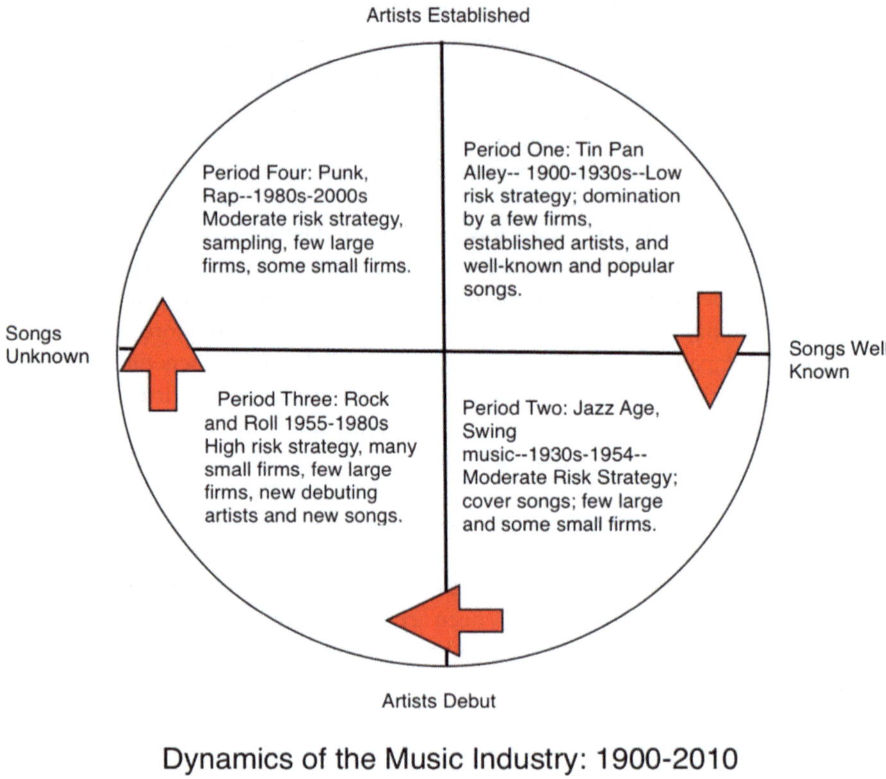

Fig. 3.1 Dynamics of the music industry, 1900–2010

actually increased them because of the wider exposure of artists on the radio. This was a period which reverts back to a less-risky strategy since there were established artists (Paul Whiteman, Benny Goodman) playing songs that had become familiar to the public through radio [142]. There continued to be a reaction against the homogenized swing sound such as with the Bebop variation on jazz, but the Majors mostly ignored these developments. The next technological change to impact the music industry came in the form of reel-to-reel tape recorders which enabled a low-cost means of building a music recording studio. This moved the industry into the high-risk Period III and the rise of rock and roll. Figure 3.2 shows what happened during the first decade of rock and roll. The number of songs making the charts rose dramatically until peaking in 1966 at 743 charting songs.

After 1955, the Majors could no longer control the number of songs released, and this created a volatile situation for their revenue streams, as Baker [9] noted. Combined with a shift toward increased music consumption by teenagers and the innovation of early rock and roll artists, the industry underwent dramatic change. This was a period of greatest uncertainty—almost the opposite of the early years of the recorded music industry.

Fig. 3.2 Total number of songs making the *Billboard* Hot 100 charts 1940–2005, *Source*: Whitburn 2002, 2006b [150, 152]

But what has happened since 1966 is a downward trend in the number of songs making the charts with a noticeable brief upsurge in the late 1990s. This downward trend began with a merger wave in 1965 as the major companies began to buy up the Indies that had emerged in the previous decade. The only Independents to survive this merger era were Motown, A & M, and a few others. The independent record companies were purchased not by other record companies but were purchased by conglomerates like RCA, CBS, and MCA. This consolidation helped the industry to return to a moderate risk strategy that was upset in the 1990s with the rise of rap and hip-hop music which again infused the industry with new music and new artists—the riskiest strategy for record companies because it creates the greatest uncertainty about success. In the past two decades, the industry has moved into Period IV where there is a moderate risk strategy.

As can be seen in Fig. 3.3, the top four songs dominate a large part of the year since 1990 when compared with the 1960s. In the past decade, rap and hip-hop have moved into the mainstream which have the effect of helping to stabilize revenues for the record companies. However, the possibilities of the Internet and cultural interaction as a result of globalization may once again foster a new period of innovation in music and the emergence once again of a risky strategy for success in the industry. The Majors will of course try to counter this and create greater stability in their revenue, but it may be difficult to do in light of the rapidity of technological change and the globalization of the world brought about through the expansion of the Internet.

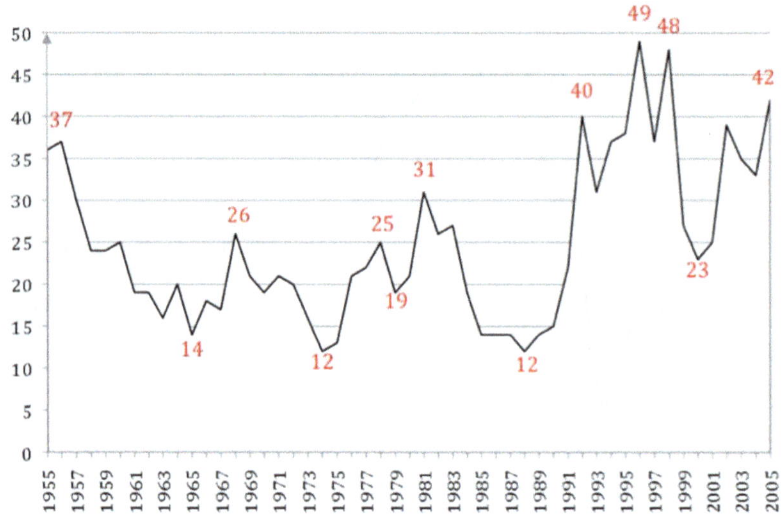

Fig. 3.3 Weeks at number 1 for top four songs of the year, 1955–2005. *Source*: Whitburn 2006a [151]

3.2 Are There Innovative Periods in Popular Music?

Given the evolution of the industry outlined above, can we identify more precisely periods of innovation? Baby boomers invariably believe that the best music was from the 1960s and that it was the most innovative period. From the discussion above, it is clear that the Majors had a profit maximizing strategy of releasing fewer records and milking those records for the maximum amount of revenue. This is a strategy that may maximize profits, but it is one that is really focused on maintaining a reliable revenue stream. In the 1950s and especially the 1960s, groups would follow up a hit song with a song that was different yet similar. Groups wanted to sound unique, and one way in which to do this is have your songs sound alike. However, groups that did this generally had shorter careers and less success. A good example of this is the group Classics IV that released "Spooky" and went to number 3, Stormy to number 5 and Traces to number 2. After the initial success of these three songs, however, none of their next eight releases made it to the top 10. What is clear is that the artists must have songs that have a distinct sound, yet you cannot redo the same song over and over.

Peterson and Berger [115] tested the hypothesis that competition and innovation go together and found that they do. From the mid-1950s to the mid-1960s, the number of firms with top ten hits increased and the big four firms concentration ratio (percentage of the hits accounted for by the largest four record companies) increased. Consider the following Fig. 3.4.

Over the period of the mid- to late-1950s, the number of firms increased and the top four firm concentration ratio decreased. The number of firms with only one hit song in the year also increased over this period as seen in Fig. 3.5. This number rose steadily between 1955 and 1959, from around 10 to 29, stayed at a high level through

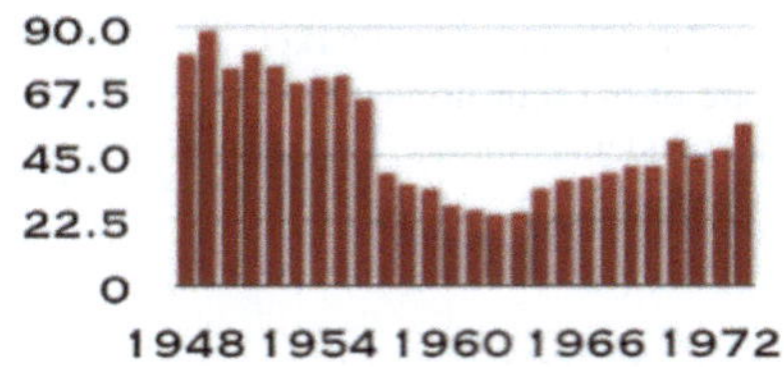

Fig. 3.4 Percentage of top ten hits by the top four firms in the recording industry 1948–1973. *Source*: Peterson and Berger 1975 [115]

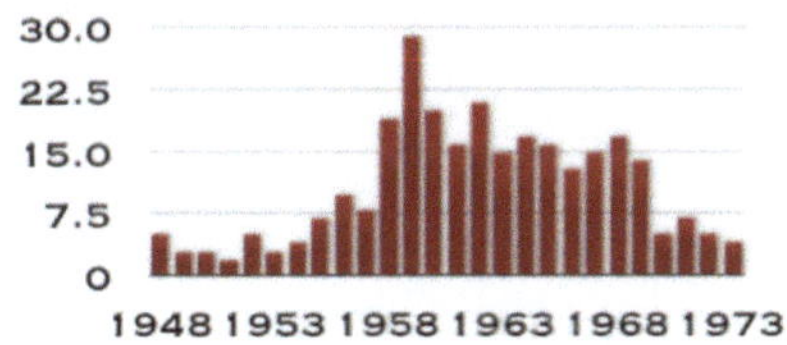

Fig. 3.5 Number of firms in the recording industry with only one hit in the top 10 1948–1973. *Source*: Peterson and Berger 1975 [115]

about 1962, and then began a fairly steady decline to under 20 by the late 1960s, but still above the pre-rock and roll era.

Lopes [99] followed up the Peterson and Berger study by looking at the period after 1974 and through the 1980s to see if the market had again reverted to the dominance of a few firms. This was indeed the case with both singles and albums. But did this also mean that innovation and diversity in musical style was inhibited as Peterson and Berger concluded about the earlier period? Lopes found that the Majors responded by increasing artist diversity. There was not a return to a period like the Big Band era when the major firms dominated the charts because they also controlled musical style. The industry did not, and probably could not, return to the low-risk strategy of Stage I where songs and artists were established by the big record companies.

The innovative genres of the 1980s were new wave/punk rock and rap. These artists were not part of the Majors but, like rock and roll in the 1950s, were mostly independent, start-up record companies. Despite the market domination by the Majors, these artists were able to break through. As digital technology and the Internet came into play in the 1990s, the problems for the big four record companies multiplied, despite their domination of the charts and the airways [72].

In the years before 1955, the big four firms accounted for 80–90% of the hits. If you look at global sales in Fig. 3.6 as an indication of concentration in the record industry today, it doesn't look much different from the pre-rock and roll years. The Majors have almost 90% of global music sales. However, the difference with the earlier periods is that the Internet and digital technology has resulted in the pie growing smaller. This is what has undermined the domination by the big four firms.

3.3 Who are the Innovative Artists?

Having identified periods where there is greater innovation, can we identify innovative artists? When asked to name the greatest and most innovative artists of the Rock and Roll Era, people will quickly name Elvis Presley, The Beatles, and

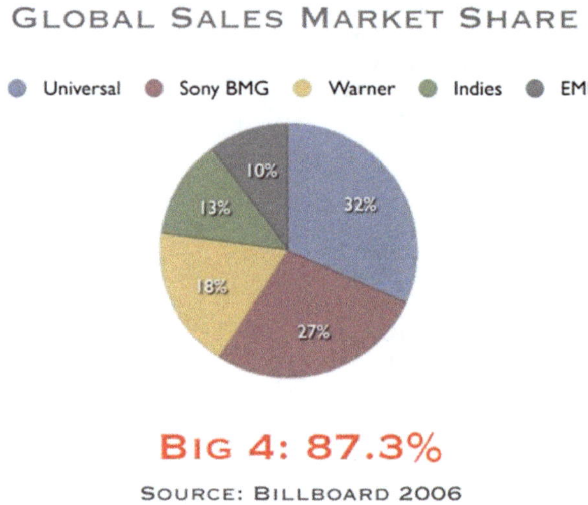

Fig. 3.6 Global sales market share of big four firms and independents. *Source*: *Billboard* 2006

then, depending on their own preferences, will give a list of many artists such as Buddy Holly, Bob Dylan, Jimi Hendrix, and numerous others. One can debate this endlessly, but the problem is to find which artists represent an impact so great that it shows up in the information from the *Billboard* charts. Undoubtedly, Buddy Holly with his innovations with the electric guitar, his musical stylings, and even his vocal styles were enormously influential on the 1960s ([133], pp. 50–51). Holly's short career due to his early death means that his impact on the charts was much less than what it might have been. Holly's only number one *Billboard* song was his first, "That'll be the Day." Many artists who would not be considered particularly influential had charting success that exceeded that of Holly. So what do the charts tell us about who are the innovative artists?

Figure 3.7 charts the number of weeks that the top or dominant artist had the number one record on the *Billboard* Hot 100 charts. In both 1956 and 1957, Elvis had the number one song for 25 weeks. Elvis was the dominant artist of the period 1956–1960 except for 1959 when he was in the Army. The Beatles dominated the period 1964–1969, except for 1966 when The Monkees were the top act. To date, Mariah Carey has been the number one artist in 4 years, peaking at 24 weeks at number one in 1995. How many would include Mariah Carey in a list of the most influential artists? When Mariah's accomplishments are compared with Elvis and The Beatles, she comes very close to their achievements in the music industry. For example, as of April 2008, she was tied with Presley for second place as the artist with the greatest number of number one hits, exceeded only by The Beatles. Can Carey be considered as innovative an artist as The Beatles and Presley?

After 1991, Nielsen SoundScan began compiling the charts on the basis of actual monitored radio play and actual point-of-sale information of mostly large retailers. During the early 1990s when Mariah Carey was the dominant artist, there was roughly

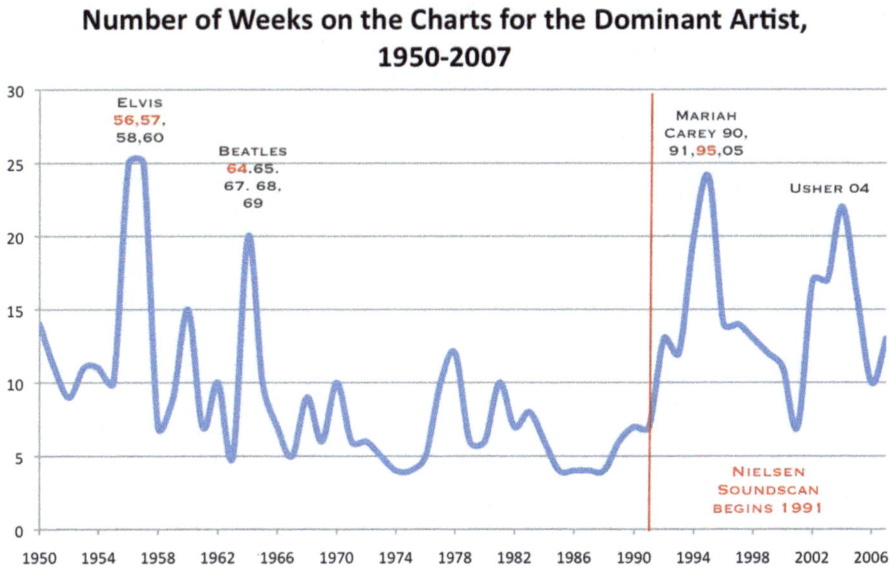

Fig. 3.7 Number of weeks on the charts by the dominant artist. *Source*: Whitburn 2006b [152]

half the number of total charting songs which means less competition. Does this diminish the accomplishments of Mariah Carey when compared with Elvis and The Beatles? It can be debated, but the facts are that the period 1955–1966 was one of increased competition and instability in the record industry. The decade of the 1990s was one of greater stability which benefited from the Majors' domination of the industry and the advent of CD technology and the rise of the "Big Box" retailers like Wal-Mart. The fact that the industry structure was quite different in the periods when Elvis Presley, The Beatles, and Mariah Carey topped the charts means that these artists may not be in the same category of artistic achievement despite similar chart success. Indeed, it suggests that other methods are necessary to identify innovative artists.

3.4 Radio, Payola and Innovation

Though one can argue about which are the innovative eras and who are the innovative artists, it is clear that the industry is cyclical. These cycles are driven by changes in technology, consumer tastes, artist creativity, and by the response of the record companies. Radio has been an important technology in the history of recorded music. In the Rock and Roll Era, independent regional AM radio stations helped create national hits in the 1950s and 1960s. This declined with the rise of FM radio and consolidation in the radio industry [108].

Radio DJs played an important role in 1950s rock and roll by promoting the sale of records instead of sheet music. The DJs selected the songs to be played on the radio and had a strong self-interest in playing the songs that they thought the teenagers would actually want to buy. Though there may have been cases of a "bad" song becoming popular, a DJ couldn't really control the preferences of teenagers despite the beliefs of various individuals in the industry or members of Congress.

The interconnectedness between the production and distribution networks (record companies and radio) resulted in charges in the late 1950s of "payola"—defined as payments made to achieve additional airplay for a recording. In a *Los Angeles Times* article of December 3, 1959, according to the then editor of *Variety*, Abner Green, the term "payola" goes back to the days of song "pluggers" who made payments to vaudeville singers to sing their songs. "Song pluggers" were employed to sing the song at various outlets, and organ grinders played the songs on the street. These pluggers, who worked for the sheet music companies, were the intermediary between the songwriter and the consuming public. Irving Caesar, an ASCAP executive director at the time, who wrote classics such as "Tea for Two" and "Just a Gigilo" acknowledged there was nothing new about payola because singers had long been paid to sing songs to live audiences in hopes of generating increased sales. However, he stated in an article in the *Los Angeles Times* of September 25, 1961 that a song presently (the 1960s) got played over and over on radio whether the public liked it or not.

Payola could be paid in various ways, but the most frequent consisted of direct cash, interest-free loans or in-kind pay-for-play payments to the DJ, adding the DJ as a song cowriter, or the DJ could own shares in a music publishing company. To provide a perspective on the income involved, consider a Detroit DJ who quit his $60,000 a year job because of the payola that was reported in the *Los Angeles Times* on November 18, 1959. The DJ said several small companies had offered him $100 a week to play their song several times a day. He claimed that several DJs were getting payments from 5 to 10 companies and making from $25,000 to $50,000 per year from such payments. He further said he could not play the music he wanted because he had to play from the charts put together by the music trade publishers. According to a *Los Angeles Times* article of February 19, 1960, *Cash Box* was the music trade publication that claimed its top ten-song list was compiled from letters sent in by DJs around the country.

In a *Los Angeles Times* article of February 10, 1960, a Cleveland DJ, Joseph Finan, making a reported $40,000 a year, said he kept an eye out for good records from certain companies and for "consideration" in playing those records he had taken $15,500 in payola over 2 years. The payola investigation involved both radio and television DJs including Dick Clark, who was the host of ABC's "American Bandstand," and Alan Freed. Though charged with taking "pay for play," Alan Freed was also listed as a cowriter on some songs. Perhaps the most financially rewarding cowriting credit Freed received was for Chuck Berry's "Nadine." Dick Clark, on the other hand, went into a far more lucrative part of the music business which was music publishing. This aligned his interests with the publishers' and did not appear as "seedy" as taking $100 to play a song on the radio. It was reported in a *Los Angeles Times* article of May 4, 1960 that Congressman Peter Mack Jr., D-IL, said at the time that it appeared to him that Clark was "the top dog in the payola field."

Ronald Coase [35] argued that the rock and roll revolution in pop music was facilitated by payola. This was partially the result of the fact that radio stations earned revenue from advertising and DJs were on salary. However, with payola, the DJ who plays a song that becomes a big hit will not only generate record sales but raise his (the DJ's) credibility with the teenage consumers. The DJ could be viewed as an entrepreneur who realized that if he could find a record by a new or unknown group and if he took ownership in the royalties, he could generate income for himself. Thus, DJs were willing to accept the risk of a possible hit by taking part ownership in a very lucrative part of the record. There was an incentive for the DJ to find the new music and not stick with what was already well established. Payola was great for the small and new bands on independent labels that had not yet broken into the industry.

Crain and Tollison [43] augment the Coase analysis by presenting evidence that changes in the structure of music were impacting the supply and demand of rock music. Specifically, they argue that the regulation of payola was not fully effective in decreasing the demand for the new rock and roll music because there was a fundamental change in the structure of music that they measured by the length and meter (number of beats-per-minute) of the music [43].

Mol and Wijnberg [104] offer an explanation for payola that places it within the dynamics of competition in a market economy. During the 1950s, given domination of radio by the Majors, the Indies adopted a strategy of using local DJs as a way to get their records on the radio. To achieve popularity with their teenage audience, the DJs wanted to play the music that teenagers liked. The DJs were filters (Mol and Wijnberg call them selectors) that enabled teenagers to hear music they viewed as "authentic"—representing the rise of the teenage culture in the 1950s. As Mol and Wijnberg note, the "local radio DJs had every incentive to provide the teenage audience with precisely this kind of (authentic) music" ([104], p. 711).

The payola scandal gained prominence in the early days of rock and roll at a time when the rise of rock and roll was viewed as leading to integration of the races in the USA that many viewed as unacceptable [126]. Though the payola issue was presented as a question of morality and corruption, it was in fact an issue about the economics of the radio industry. Payola served to promote innovation, as Coase noted, and thus helped promote the rise of rock and roll. This is the underlying economic reason that it was attacked by some.

3.5 Radio Monopoly: Clear Channel

In recent years, the company Clear Channel has purchased radio stations in the major markets in the USA covering all types of music. In doing so, the purpose is to have demographically defined consumers for each market to then sell advertising to companies. The playlists, which Clear Channel does not make available, reflect tastes in music that are well known and have a reliable demand. Clear Channel owns over 1,200 stations and dominates in many major markets. Though radio played an

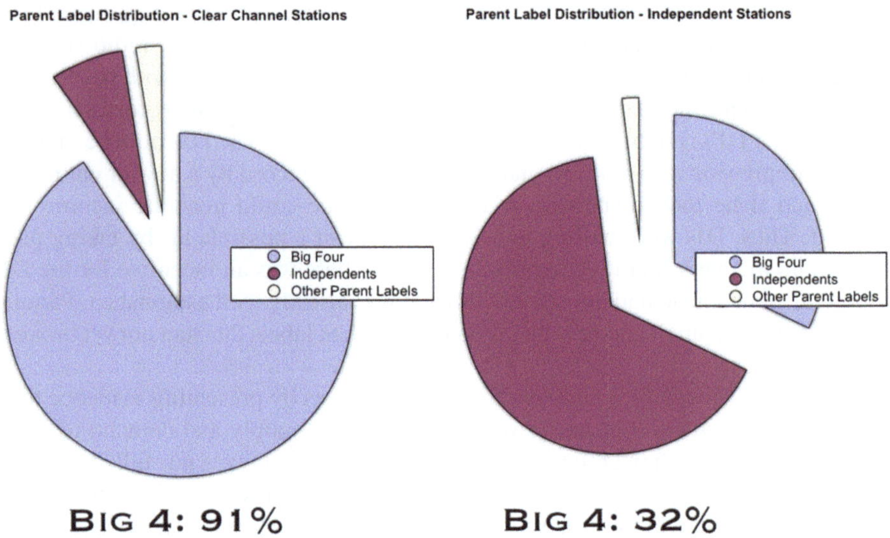

Fig. 3.8 Comparison of a sample of clear channel and independent radio station playlists

important role in the Big Band era and again with rock and roll, today some have questioned the future of terrestrial radio especially in light of its domination by large firms such as Clear Channel. Instead of promoting innovation, radio is reinforcing the status quo in terms of musical style.

A sample was taken of Clear Channel stations and independent stations and evaluated for whether they were playing songs from the big four firms (Universal, Sony BMG, Warner, and EMI). As can be seen in Fig. 3.8, Clear Channel playlists were dominated by the big four firms—91% of their playlists. In contrast, only 32% of the songs on the playlists of a sample of independent stations were from the big four firms. Playing new and innovative music is not characteristic of Clear Channel-owned radio stations, and they are producing for a mass audience and not those seeking innovative music. This seeming monopoly on the airwaves was countered by the emergence of music television in 1981 with MTV, though it quickly became dominated by the major firms. The availability of music on the Internet and the streaming of radio stations both independent and Clear Channel provides additional choice in music. The rejection of radio standardization of playlists has likely been one factor that has spurred the distribution of music on the Internet and consumers burning their own CDs with the music that reflects their tastes. It may well be that radio will again play an important role in music innovation. The Internet allows you to go global, but what is needed today is the equivalent of the song pluggers of the late nineteenth and early twentieth centuries.

Who are the song pluggers for the Age of the Internet? These are the companies such as Rhapsody, Pandora, the now Apple-owned Lala.com, Spotify, and others that seek to gather data on what consumers like in music and then provide information on other music they might like. Tom Petty wrote a song "The Last DJ" about the impact of Clear Channel's monopoly on the "freedom of choice" for listeners to hear new music selected by a DJ. However, it may be that music consumers are more willing to trust a favorite DJ who broadcasts over Internet radio, or satellite services like SiriusXM, than a piece of software. This could lead to a resurgence of DJs and a return to the role that radio has played in the history of recorded music, namely bringing new and innovative music to a mass audience. Rather than DJs disappearing, it is possible that they may again play a prominent role in helping consumers find innovative music. With more and more music available on a global basis, some way to find the most that an individual consumer likes must be found. Though iTunes offers its "Genius" button, people may prefer and trust the recommendations of a live DJ.

3.6 Innovation in Music: What is New, is Old

Will you ever hear surf music again? Judging from an examination of the evolution of modern music, the answer is yes. The reason is that new music always contains an element of the music that preceded it. Psychologists like Daniel Levitin [93] have studied music as a "human obsession." Though they may disagree about what is "good" music, there is no doubt that music has been an essential element in being human. It is also the case that there are reasons why certain music seems to transcend generations and genres. Those tunes are the ones that successfully innovate and create something new but retain an element of familiarity.

This process of continual innovation in musical style results in a rather tumultuous industry in modern times. The reason is that those supplying music cannot expect to have a steady income stream over a long period of time. This is because consumer tastes change, artists create something new, and technology evolves. The Majors responded to the rise of rock and roll through acquiring independent firms and in changing the way they did business, for example, now catering to teenagers. The difference between the situation the Majors find themselves in today compared with the 1960s is that the Majors no longer have a monopoly on how the music gets produced and distributed. Adjusting to the Digital and Internet Age will require a more fundamental change in the way the Majors operate than it did beginning in the 1960s. Whether or not they will be able to adjust is not known at present, but history suggests that they will change their way of doing business. One thing is clear and that is the record company as we knew it in the twentieth century will not be part of the twenty-first.

Chapter 4
Contracts: You Never Give Me Your Money, All I Get Is Your Funny Paper

Lawyers love the music industry. If you put the words "musicians" and "sue" into a Google search you get over three million hits. Though not a direct measure of legal problems that arise in the music industry, it does provide some indication of the extent to which the music industry is riddled with lawsuits that are invariably about the contracts that are signed in the industry. One party sues the other for failure to fulfill the terms of the contract. Record companies sue artists, artists sue record companies and publishing companies, and band members sue each other [31].

A good example of the latter is the case of the Beach Boys. The group was originally formed in 1961 and was comprised of three brothers, a cousin, and a friend. The Wilson brother's father was the manager. The original group barely made it out of the 1960s as a recording and live performance group primarily due to the problems of the main composer for the group, Brian Wilson, who is the only surviving brother. The other two original members of the group, Mike Love and Al Jardine, have recently reached a settlement with Brian Wilson that will enable all three to continue touring and possibly a reunion of the three surviving members. The long court battle came about because Jardine was touring under the name "Beach Boys Family and Friends" until a federal judge ruled in 2000 that this was an infringement on the Beach Boys trademark for which Mike Love was the only one licensed under a deal negotiated in 1998 with the band's corporate identity, Brothers Records—a corporation that is jointly owned by Brian Wilson, Jardine, Love, and the estate of Carl Wilson. The decision was upheld by a U.S. appeals court in 2003. Subsequently in 2004, Mike Love and the Carl Wilson estate sued Jardine for $2.2 million in legal fees and this was the case that was settled in 2008. In 2012, the surviving members of the band, backed with additional musicians, embarked on a 50th anniversary reunion tour.

The group Smashing Pumpkins sued their label, Virgin Records, in March 2008 for illegal use of the band's name and music in promotional deals with Pepsi that impact the band's "goodwill" with fans. The band contends that they never granted Virgin the right to use the band's name in promotional campaigns. The lawsuit asks that Virgin turn over profits from the promotion to the band and there be an injunction against any future use of the band's name or music in future promotional campaigns.

R.J. Phillips, *Rock and Roll Fantasy?: The Reality of Going from Garage Band to Superstardom*, SpringerBriefs in Business 35, DOI 10.1007/978-1-4614-5900-2_4,

Stone Temple Pilots has had problems mostly connected to drug abuse by one of the band members, Scott Weiland. In June 2008, Atlantic Records sued the band because they owe the company a seventh album and possibly two more beyond that. The group effectively quit performing in 2002 and only recently reunited in 2008 for a national tour. Atlantic contends that the contract with the band was written under New York state law and that the band was trying to use California state law to terminate the contract. The lawsuit seeks a court declaration of its rights under the recording contract and recovery of legal fees. The band has not been on the charts since 2000, but they have reunited and began touring in 2010.

The surviving members of the 1960s group The Doors are also having problems. The four original members of the band, whose lead singer and lyricist Jim Morrison died in 1970, signed an agreement that any business deal would require unanimous consent. This meant that any one member had veto power over any actions taken by the band. The agreement among the band members originally came about because Buick wanted to use a Doors' song but Morrison objected. In recent years, Densmore has objected to the use of Doors' music by General Motors to sell Cadillacs and Apple for an iPod commercial. Keyboardist Ray Manzarek and guitarist Robby Krieger were ordered to pay $5 million to the drummer John Densmore and Jim Morrison's parents for improperly using The Doors' name when the pair toured as "The Doors of the 21st Century" with Ian Astbury, formerly of The Cult, as the lead singer. In 2002, Densmore, who declined an offer to tour with Manzarek and Kreiger, objected to the band use of the name on the grounds that without the deceased Morrison, they shouldn't use the name. The tour grossed $8 million and netted $3.2 million and was not distributed to either Densmore or the Morrison estate.

In his book *This Business of Urban Music*, James L. Walker discusses numerous examples of contracts gone bad. In the 1990s, Prince, who had signed a contract with Warner Brothers allowing them to retain ownership of his masters, began appearing on media outlets with the word "slave" printed on his face. His first album after getting out of the contract was released in 1996 and titled *Emancipation*. The late rap star Tupac Shakur died in 1996 never having had a music lawyer. After his death, his label released albums, froze the royalty payments, and kept their profits. According to a lawyer later retained by Tupac's mother, there was over $13 million in frozen royalty payments that belonged to Tupac [144].

From such stories, it makes one think that if you want to get involved with the music industry you might be better off being a lawyer than a musician. The common denominator is that there are problems whenever contracts are drawn up. The key question is whether contracts can be better designed to avoid the legal fees. Though in a less than perfect world, some litigation will remain; these disputes do nothing to improve the quantity and quality of music available to consumers. The premise of this chapter is that everyone would be better off if contracts could be designed to minimize the incentive to break them. Though lawyers benefit from litigation, they could probably benefit even more from better contracts and better negotiations. This chapter discusses the economics of contracts and discusses how technology has changed contracts in the digital age.

4.1 Contracts in the Music Industry

Economists have long extolled the virtues of free competitive markets. However, Oliver Williamson was awarded the Nobel Prize in economics in part for his recognition that in the modern economy, contracts are an important way in which goods and services are exchanged. Building on the work of John R. Commons, an economist who wrote in the first decades of the twentieth century, Williamson argued that transactions are the key unit to be analyzed in the economy and often times the transactions are more complex than traditional economic theory might suggest. The essence of the problem is twofold. First, though people try to act in their own self-interest, because of uncertainty about what will happen in the future and a lack of information resources available and outcomes, they will be unable to do as economists have theorized. In economists' jargon people are "boundedly rational." They seek the best they can do in furthering their own self-interest given available information and the organizations and institutions they must operate within. Further, a self-interest motivation may also guide people to lie, steal, and cheat. Given these two problems, transactions between two parties can be quite costly. There may be a need for some monitoring mechanism—a way for each to keep tabs on the other—on the parties or a third party to ensure both parties live up to their contract. It is also apparent that many contracts may end up in the legal system and decisions will be made by the courts, and, of course, lawyers will be paid to provide legal counsel. Williamson's analysis is readily applicable to the music industry.

As noted in an earlier chapter, friends who form bands typically assume that everyone is equal and that the net revenues (after expenses) are divided equally among the band members. However, it may also be the case that the member who owns the P.A. system may get a little more to compensate for his additional expenditure. This works as long as the band is just a cover band doing local gigs. Things change if the band tries to go to the next step and write their own songs and actually try to earn a living from creating new music. This requires a contract of some sort being written and signed by the band members. This could be a contract with a manager (Colonel Parker in Elvis's case and Brian Epstein for The Beatles) or it could be a contract with a record company. The contract specifies the band's obligations and the rewards that it will receive in fulfilling its contract.

The reason the history of rock and roll is replete with ill-conceived contracts and resultant royalty disputes is because the basic problem is the uncertainty of whether any particular artist or any particular recording will be bought by the public. Of course, this in itself is no different than providing any other good or service in a market economy. If no one wants the product you are selling, you won't be in business long. What is special about the music industry? Even though producing music is not like producing cars, it is like other entertainment industries and sports. Historically, the music industry has been characterized as one where large investments are needed to develop and promote artists and the probability of having a hit is usually low. The music industry, like sports, depends on contracts with uncertain outcomes.

It is not easy to get detailed information on contracts. Obviously, they are confidential agreements and there is no reason why they should be public information. Neither party has an incentive to release the full information publicly; however, it is not unusual for at least some of the details of contracts to be revealed in the popular media. These details must come from one of the parties involved in the contract. Presumably when artists enter contract negotiations, especially where a successful artist is renegotiating an earlier contract, there is more information available to both parties about what other comparable artists are getting, even if the full details of all contracts are not publicly disclosed.

The first observation about recording contracts is to note that most of them end up broken. The problem is that if an artist is successful, then he or she wants to renegotiate to receive greater compensation. If the artist is a failure, then the record company wants out of the contract. In one of the few available studies about contracts, Steven Wildman [155] examined over 600 contracts signed over the years 1994–2000 between artists and the five major music groups. His principal findings were that (1) the odds of success for a new artist were very low, (2) labels invest considerable sums to record and market albums by unproven artists, and (3) artists who have a hit album renegotiate their contracts and require significant additional upfront commitments by the record labels. The study was funded by the Recording Industry Association of America (RIAA), but in my view, this in no way biases the Wildman study.

The Wildman study is quite valuable in understanding the economics of contracts in the music industry and the information contained is useful for both sides of a recording contract. Assuming his sample is representative, he concludes that about three-quarters of artists signed to contracts will release albums 5–7 years later, but only about 10% will still be under contract after 5–7 years. This is consistent with the data on chart survival rates of groups discussed earlier, though success on the charts typically declines near the end of the charting career. The average upfront commitment (execution advance plus recording funds) for a first album in a contract in the period 1994–1996 was nearly $300,000 in year 2000 dollars. For similar contracts signed in 2000, this figure had risen to over $450,000 ([155], pp. 9–10).

The Wildman study also provides information on the complex and multifaceted aspects of recording contracts. There is no such thing as a "standard" contract and there is substantial variation in contract terms among newly signed artists ([155], p. 13). The number of albums potentially required to be delivered over the contract varied between 1 and 10, and royalties ranged from 4 to 20% with a mean of 15.2% ([155], p. 17). Upfront commitments by the companies for the newly signed artists ranged from $25,000 to over $1,000,000.

Wildman notes that contracts of artists who have hit records are typically renegotiated. In his study he found that the average upfront advance for new artists was $450,000 but went up to $3.7 million for those who renegotiated their contracts. This confirms that there is little possibility of an "optimal" recording contract because demand is uncertain and the payoff is unknown. The RIAA would look at the results of Wildman's study and want people to conclude that they are in a very risky business with a low return and that they are being taken advantage of by artists once they are successful. In their view, the record companies spend huge amounts on unknown artists, most of whom do not produce hits, and when they do, the company does not reap the full benefits. The question is why should they? This is the way the game of risk is played in the music industry. If you aren't earning sufficient profits, you should probably get into another industry. However, it is human nature to try and maintain a steady income stream. That's hard to do in competitive industries, especially those in the entertainment area.

The basic problem in negotiating a recording contract can be illustrated by noting its similarity to a lottery. Investing in an artist is taking a gamble and how do we determine the fair market price of a gamble? Consider the following example. Suppose there is a lottery where the probability is 1% of a payoff of \$1,000,000 and a probability of 99% of a zero payoff. The expected or mean payoff is $0.01 \times \$1{,}000{,}000 = \$10{,}000$. Would anyone pay \$10,000 for this lottery? Obviously not. What is a more realistic price? Perhaps \$1. The price is determined by whether the individual is a risk lover or risk avoider, the wealth of the individual, and any potential bargaining with whoever is selling the lottery.

Burke [22] analyzes the structure of the music industry by devising a model that has the band member (who is also a composer in his model) make a choice between licensing the compositions with an existing record company or through the formation of her own company. The main determinants of this decision are (1) differences in the estimation of the value of the composition between the composer and the record company, (2) whether the composer has alternative companies to sign with or if the company feels it cannot "lock-in" the composer, (3) whether the composer likes to avoid taking too much risk, (4) wealth constraint, (5) whether the record considers introducing a new artist to be a good thing or economies of scale for the record company, and (6) record company profits. Using a data set from Irish musicians, Burke finds that musicians seek contracts with record companies rather than create their own companies because of the expense involved. Composers who start up their own company usually do so because of "push" rather than "pull" factors so that such new firm formation is mainly accounted for by artistic enterprise rejected by incumbent firms. In this manner, new firm formation by composers does not appear to represent the seeds of future industrial growth ([22], p. 471).

But Burke reached his conclusion from data in the 1990s and technology and the Internet have lowered the cost of producing a record, though the distribution—getting someone to hear the music—remains a problem. Still, given the general importance of entrepreneurship to an economy, resources could be usefully applied to increasing the entrepreneurial abilities of composers or musicians in general. With greater training in business, musicians could avoid the exploitation that many groups experienced. As Mick Jagger put it:

> I'll never forget the deals I did in the 60s, which were just terrible. You say, Oh, I'm a creative person, I won't worry about this. But that just doesn't work. Because everyone would just steal every penny you've got ([127], p. 71).

Efforts to maintain control over the songs they have written is a long-standing problem in the music industry. A closer examination of Buddy Holly's experience is illustrative of the issues involved.

4.2 Buddy Holly's Contracts

The first contract that Buddy Holly signed was to have Hipockets Duncan be the manager of Buddy, Bob Montgomery, and Larry Welborn who performed around Lubbock, Texas, as "The Buddy and Bob Show." Duncan was a local radio DJ and he booked the group for local gigs in and around Lubbock. When the group became successful enough to play outside of the west Texas area, Duncan said that he would tear up the contract and end his role. When the country and western division of Decca Records offered Holly a contract to record in Nashville, Duncan did as he promised without any further financial remuneration and the contract was ended. However, things were quite different after Holly signed with Decca.

The first thing is that Decca only offered a contract to Holly and not to the members of his band. The trio broke up and Holly recruited new musicians to go with him to the Nashville recording session: Sonny Curtis on lead guitar, Jerry Allison on drums, and Don Guess on standup bass guitar. Holly and his group recorded a number of records at his two Nashville recording sessions including a version of "That'll Be the Day." None of the Holly releases were successful on the country and western charts and Decca was planning on releasing Holly from his 5-year contract which gave the company the option each year of continuing or dropping the contract and they did so after 1 year [69].

The failure at Decca was fortuitous for Holly because it led him to a visit to Clovis, New Mexico, and the recording studio of independent producer, Norman Petty. With his own trio, Petty had some chart success and opened the studio in 1955 in his hometown. Petty's trio was under contract to one of the major companies, Columbia, and Petty had close ties with Mitch Miller and Murray Deutch who ran Peer-Southern Music publishing company. Petty ran his operation differently than the major companies. Rather than charge by the hour, Petty charged by the song. He stated that it was his experience as an artist that producing a quality product took time. The biggest cost in doing this was the cost of Petty's time in producing the record. The cost of the materials needed to make the recording (tape, electricity) was very low, though not zero. However, Petty had his own music publishing company and in compensation for the recording costs, the songs recorded in his studio were typically published by Nor-Va-Jak or later, Dundee.

For the Clovis sessions and the contract with Petty, Holly formed a new band which included Niki Sullivan on guitar to replace Sonny Curtis and Joe B. Mauldin on bass. The name of the group that would sign the contract with Petty was The Crickets. Because Holly had not yet been officially released from his Decca contract and it forbid him from re-recording any of the songs he had done for Decca for 5 years, it was decided that the formation of a group that omitted Holly's name would be the best strategy for dealing with any potential contract problems with Decca Records. Holly was convinced that "That'll Be the Day" could be a hit with the new version recorded in Clovis.

Petty played the tape of "That'll Be the Day" for Bob Thiele, A&R director for Coral Records. A meeting was set up by Murray Deutch who wanted half of the publishing rights for "That'll Be the Day" for his company Peer-Southern in exchange for help getting a record contract for The Crickets. The contract was with Brunswick Records, an independent subsidiary of Decca. That the contract ended up being indirectly with Decca was purely an accident, but one that saved some lawsuits after "That'll Be the Day" was a hit. After the Brunswick version was a hit, Decca required Holly to waive any royalties due to him on sales of the original Nashville recording.

There was still one problem and that was who would have the publishing rights for "That'll Be the Day." Originally it had been published by Cedarwood and the company threatened to sue Petty and Nor-Va-Jak over the copyright of the song. The deal Petty worked was to give Cedarwood the copyright to a future Holly song ("Think it Over") in exchange for the full copyright of "That'll be the Day" remaining with Nor-Va-Jak.

Though the Crickets were signed to the Decca subsidiary Brunswick, Holly had a separate contract with Coral records, another Decca subsidiary. Holly could release records either under his name on Coral or with the group on Brunswick. It was thought that this might be a way to increase the number of releases for Holly since DJs might be reluctant to play two songs by the same artist. Holly was one of the first artists to have this arrangement and a decade later Frankie Valli of the Four Seasons followed this model ([69], p. 58).

Though Holly first insisted that all revenues of the band be shared equally, Petty evidently convinced the group that an equal split for gigs was reasonable, but not for recording. When the group became a trio, Holly took 50% and Allison and Mauldin each received 25%. On record royalties, Holly received 65% whether it was a solo record or with the Crickets. The contracts with Coral and Brunswick called for Holly and the Crickets to receive a mechanical royalty of 5% (calculated as 5% times 90% of the retail price of the record). This rate was above the 1 or 2% many rock and roll artists were receiving at the time.

The 1978 movie "The Buddy Holly Story" did not include any mention of Petty. The argument is made by some that the contract that Holly signed with Petty was "unfair" in the sense of unduly rewarding Petty for his contributions to Holly's success. In a larger context, the dispute between Holly and Petty was really about how to establish an equitable artist/record company relationship under the changed technological and institutional environment of rock and roll. Unfortunately, but understandable for both personal and historical reasons, Holly and Petty were not able to come to agreement. However, it is far from clear that Norman Petty was inordinately to blame for this failure. Both Petty and Holly were innovators in the production of music, but they were not able to forge a business model together. This model was based on a division of labor in the production of music and an established technology for distributing the music. It has taken the emergence of digital technology and the Internet to force changes in the traditional business model that dominated most of the twentieth century.

Because Holly was strapped financially due to the legal battles over his royalties, and with a wife who was expecting a child, Holly was compelled to go on the Winter Dance Party tour. One can only contemplate the impact on the development of rock and roll if Petty and Holly had managed to agree to a "fair" contract or resolved their differences.

4.3 Why Did the Beatles Break Up?

The most famous band breakup of all time was of course The Beatles. Numerous books have been written about why the group broke up, but there is no doubt that the contract they signed was no longer working well for the group. Though you can blame Yoko Ono, it's more likely the inability of George Harrison to get more songs on an album was of greater significance. If The Beatles had been able to do what Buddy Holly did—sign separate contracts for the group and as solo artists—The Beatles might have stayed together. Today artists have greater control over their careers and there is more opportunity to record with a group, as a solo, or just record duets with another solo artist.

Though the chart success of The Beatles far exceeds that of the average group or solo artist, superstars like Mariah Carey are approaching some of The Beatles' chart records. As of 2006, The Beatles had 20 number one songs on the *Billboard* Hot 100, 34 in the top 10, and 72 chartings songs over a charting career lasting from 1964 to 1996. Mariah Carey, for a charting career from 1990 to 2006, had 17 number ones, 26 in the top 10, and 40 in the top 100. But what if The Beatles had not broken up or had contracts which allowed them to record as solo artists? If you add the chart success of The Beatles to the chart success of Paul McCartney, John Lennon, George Harrison, and Ringo Starr, you have 36 number one songs, 74 in the top 10, and 72 in the top 100 for the charting career from 1964 to 2005. This chart success will not likely be challenged anytime in the near future. Some argue that Mariah Carey has benefited from the fact that presently there are far fewer songs making it to number one. One other comparison is that with the Rolling Stones who have had a charting career thus far from 1965 to 2003 with 8 number ones, 22 top ten, and 57 in the top 100.

Much has been written about The Beatles' involvement in music publishing. Lennon and McCartney were undoubtedly the greatest songwriting team in popular music history. Though their contract structure was innovative, ultimately others have benefited greatly from the songs that Lennon and McCartney wrote. The essence of the story is that the early Beatles' songs were published by Northern Songs which was a company owned 51% by Dick James Music and 49% split 20% each to Lennon and McCartney and the remaining 9% to North End Music Store (NEMS)—the company owned by The Beatles' manager, Brian Epstein. This contract was an innovation because for the first time songwriters had an equity share in music publishing beyond their songwriting royalties. Northern Songs also published many of George Harrison's early songs, but Harrison was not an equity owner like Lennon and McCartney.

To avoid heavy taxes in the UK, Northern Songs went public in 1965 and this, of course, led to the possibility that any particular individual could increase his or her shares and the company could be taken over by another company. Dick James, as a major shareholder, became concerned about the breakup of The Beatles and how this would affect the stock value of Northern Songs. Eventually, Associated Television Corporation (ATV) purchased enough stock in Northern Songs to gain control of the company. Lennon and McCartney together held 30% of the stock which they sold to ATV. In the 1980s when ATV was on the market, there was a chance for Lennon's widow and McCartney to buy back the songs they had written. The story is a long and winding road, but the bottom line seems to be a question of how much people thought the catalogue was worth. In the end, Michael Jackson, who had just reaped the income from his *Thriller* album, paid $47.5 million dollars to buy ATV, a figure that many, including Yoko Ono and McCartney, thought was too high. At the time of his death in 2009, Michael Jackson's share of The Beatles' catalogue was valued at around $500 million.

Today, the publishing royalties on the early Beatles songs are split 25% to McCartney, 25% to Yoko Ono, and 50% to Michael Jackson's estate and Sony Music [130]. One lesson that Paul McCartney learned from his experience as a songwriter is the importance of songwriting royalties. In July 1976, McCartney purchased the Edwin H. Morris Music catalogue which included the publishing rights to Nor-Va-Jak Music and many Buddy Holly songs.

4.4 Economics of Contracts

It is probably not an overstatement to say that the source of most of the legal problems and the breakups of groups is centered on the contract with the record company that the group signs. Solo artists also sign contracts that often end in problems, but the additional complication is that the group is made up of individuals with somewhat differing interests and different contributions to the output of the group.

I will not attempt to deliver a full treatise on the economics of contracts but rather provide some essentials to help understand the problems with contracts in the past and provide a guideline for contracts in the future. Though any economic transaction between two parties can be viewed as a contract, we are specifically interested in contracts between artists and labels or artists and managers. The contract specifies each party's obligation in providing a good or service to the other party involved in the contract. In modern society, most contracts are legally enforceable in a court of law. From an economic perspective, the problem with resorting to legal enforcement is the costs that must be paid. It is not only an expense borne by each party to the transaction but also represents a loss to society as a whole. The way to minimize the costs of enforcing a contract is to construct a contract in which both parties will have the incentive to fulfill their obligations in the contract.

Getting both parties to fulfill their respective obligations requires a structure of the contract in which both parties act honestly while each seeks their own best self-interest. To do so without resorting to a third party to monitor the contract requires disclosure and transparency between the two parties. It also requires that any asymmetries in information between the parties be minimized. In other words, if one party knows something the other party does not, then the party with the information is at an advantage. It may also be the case that the two parties do not enter into the contract as equals. This obviously is a problem when the two parties are an unknown, unproven artist and an established record company. However, once an artist is established as commercially viable, then the power relationship may be reversed. Since most contracts are made when power relations are not equal, most contracts are problematic and will be broken or one party will want to renegotiate. Where companies make the greatest profit is on an unknown artist who hits it big. This means that the record companies are like venture capitalists and they do take great risks. The corollary is that companies do not make as much profit off of established artists because of the strengthened bargaining position of the artist. The major recording companies also often find it is cheaper to let an independent firm discover an artist and then buy up the contract. This is what happened with Elvis Presley and his contract with Sam Phillips of Sun Records and RCA-Victor. Alternatively, the Majors have to spend money developing the artist and that is where it is risky.

From this brief review of the economics of contracts, it is easy to see why problems often arise and why the music industry has been very good to lawyers. Of course, the world is not perfect and there is no such thing as a contract that would eliminate all problems that might arise between two parties. However, it is also the case that the rise of the Internet and low-cost recording and distribution definitely undermines the relationship between artists and record companies that characterized most of the twentieth century. If use of the Internet is able to reduce the costs of enforcing and monitoring contracts, then it will have played an important role in improving the allocation of resources in society as a whole [45].

The use of "rules of thumb" such as the long-established 50–50 split between songwriters and music publishing companies may be cost minimizing in that they avoid negotiation on a case-by-case basis, but this does not mean that such a rule of thumb is economically efficient. Contracts could also be written so that they can be renegotiated whenever circumstances change. This, of course, raises transaction costs as well.

4.5 Contemporary Examples of Recording Contracts: Innovation

As venture capitalists, record companies have advanced the funds to promote artists and hope for a return on that investment. The costs of producing a hit song or successful artists have been tied to recording costs, touring, and promotion or advertising. The computer age has brought down recording costs significantly to the extent that many long-established recording studios are now out of business.

Corporate sponsorship is the norm for touring. This would seem to leave one important function for record companies and that would be promotion. In other words, there is still a need for a "song plugger."

Brian Message, the manager of the group Radiohead, has created a venture called Polyphonic. Radiohead has sought to use the Internet to its advantage and has experimented with offering its music online and allowing consumers to pay whatever they wish. Polyphonic is a company that will invest money in new and rising artists who have yet to sign record contracts and help promote them over the Internet. Under the model, bands will be start-up companies that record their own music and handle their publicity, merchandise, and touring. Rather than the traditional advance from recording companies, which must be recouped before bands become profitable, the band members will share in all of the profits from music and touring as well as retaining ownership of their master recordings. Polyphonic was begun with $20 million in seed financing and plans on investing around $300,000 in each band. Though the founders tried, they were unable to raise money from venture capitalists in Silicon Valley who were skeptical of the business model.

Another company that is in the works called Self Serve is been developed by Marc Geiger, an agent at William Morris Endeavor. Though details are emerging, the plan calls for providing tools and financing for artists to create business models that do not depend on the major labels.

Yet another recent innovation is what has been called "360 deals" ([111], p. 95). The deals have been prompted by the fall in mechanical royalties from record sales which were the primary source of income for the labels. From the labels' perspective, they argue that their investment in the artist creates an image and that image can be sold for endorsements, for example. Why shouldn't the label share in those revenues? Of course, once labels begin these kinds of deals, and given the change in the economics of recording production (lower costs, more vertical integration) then this means that the labels are no longer record companies, but are in the brand-building business ([111], p. 95). The problem for the labels is that they are now in a different line of business and other firms can compete with them. As an example, the touring company Live Nation signed Madonna to a multiyear, multimillion dollar deal. Just as technology and the reward system in the music industry have led artists to become singers, songwriters, producers, label owners, and so on, the record labels are now becoming companies that are not just focused on their expertise in producing records. Will record companies be able to move into new business areas and maintain profitability?

If artists no longer need the recording studio, why don't they just cut deals with Pepsi for promotion? This is the problem that record labels will have to face if they continue to push 360 deals. According to Passman, in current 360 deals the record companies are getting from 10 to 35% of the artists' net income from non-record sources, with the majority of the deals in the 20–30% range ([111], p. 96). Though receiving a percent of the artist's non-record revenue, the record companies usually only have a passive interest, meaning that they do not actively try to get involved in the artist's decisions about other revenue generating ventures. As Passman notes, the high-profile deals of Madonna and Jay-Z are really just banking transactions in the sense that the company pays a guaranteed amount to the artist for a share of touring, recording, sponsorship, branding, and so on. Seen in this light, it confirms that basically any firm with the cash on hand and the desire can cut 360 deals with artists. In 2011, Pete Townshend of The Who, noting that music publishing had always been a "form of banking," suggested that Apple's iTunes take a greater role in investing in artists. Presently iTunes was only involved in the distribution of recordings and the payment of royalties. They could also take over the roles for artists that were previously done by record companies in providing editorial guidance, financial support, creative nurture, manufacturing, publishing, and marketing [140]. This development may lead to a more rapid decline in specialized record companies.

4.6 Catastrophic Insurance for Record Companies?

The basic principles of insurance are well understood. A company will offer to insure risks—life, auto, home—and will charge premiums that cover the expected losses plus a profit for the company. Actuarial tables and other data enable companies to offer insurance on the risk of dying at a certain age, the risk of your house burning down or of your having a wreck in your car, and so on. For all of these outcomes there is some reasonably well-known probability of the events. Premiums reflect the risk assessment and if the insurance company is well managed, they stay in business.

Record companies can purchase insurance on the success or failure of a particular artist if they feel the risks are so high that the added expense of insurance would be worth it. Dick James took out a million dollar life insurance policy on Lennon and McCartney in the early days of Northern Songs. Certainly Live Nation, when it signed the contract with Madonna for a multiyear deal, took out insurance on the possibility of her not being able to fulfill her obligations because of death or injury. AEG Live, the company that was promoting Michael Jackson's series of fifty concerts, bought insurance to cover losses in the event that Jackson was unable to perform. Though obviously you can't insure for potential profits, according to AEG Live CEO Randy Phillips, the company did insure its "hard costs" in the amount of $20 to $25 million. In that case, AEG Live also owns other assets related to Jackson's planned concerts that will generate revenue as well.

If record companies want to argue that there is fundamental uncertainty about whether an artist will be successful or not and that regular insurance would not work, there is always the catastrophic or reinsurance industry. This is an industry where someone like Warren Buffet's Berkshire Hathaway is involved. The catastrophic insurance industry is usually for natural disasters. In those cases, both the probability of the event and the amount of losses are basically unknown and cannot be reasonably calculated on the basis of any probability tables. This market is basically a gamble or a bet between two parties. When Buffet's company buys a catastrophic insurance contract, it is making a bet on whether a disaster occurs.

If no disaster occurs, the company gets a large payment. If a disaster does occur, the company has a large payout. I do not know of any examples of record companies seeking to enter the catastrophic insurance industry as a way to hedge their potential losses. This may be due to the fact that no one is willing to accept the other side of the bet, or that there is not as fundamental uncertainty about record success as earthquakes. In that case, the regular insurance market, as used by AEG Live in the Jackson situation, could be utilized.

Chapter 5
Live Performance: Touring Can Make You Crazy. Are Your Grandparents Driving Up Ticket Prices?

When I tell my students that I paid $4 to hear Jimi Hendrix in 1970, they are astonished. Even in 2009 dollars, that is only $22. In 1965, you could have seen The Beatles at Shea Stadium for $5. The average ticket price for a recent Paul McCartney tour was $121.57. McCartney played three concerts to open Citi Field—the replacement for Shea Stadium—in July 2009. There were 150,000 tickets sold for the three concerts and the cheapest tickets were $49.50. According to FanSnap, the average ticket price on the secondary market was $194.70. Even if you adjust for inflation, the 1965 Shea Stadium tickets would only be $33 in today's prices. The price of seeing Paul McCartney has quadrupled over four decades? Why have ticket prices risen so much faster than inflation? There are two primary reasons. The first is that entertainment costs have risen faster than the prices of goods and services in other sectors. These are the costs of putting on a concert and range from the costs of venue rental, increased labor costs, and an expansion of the production values in the concert—you are getting more than just musical entertainment from lavish sets and better sound. Second, while it is unlikely that there was a big change in teenagers wanting to go to rock and roll concerts, clearly their post-World War II-generation parents and grandparents who grew up with groups like The Beatles still attend concerts. Teenagers who could only afford $5 in 1965 are now adults who have higher incomes and can afford $200 for concert tickets. This effect has been called the "boomer effect" on ticket prices.

Rock and roll concerts today are light years away from those of the 1950s and 1960s. Though the prices were cheap, the performances were not of high quality despite having talented performers. They were often not well organized and the consumers or fans did not really get a lot for their money and the artists generally did not earn a lot while on the road if it was a record company sponsored tour. To illustrate the problems of touring in the early days of rock and roll it is instructive to begin with a look at the most infamous rock and roll tour ever: the 1959 Winter Dance Party. This tour, in the middle of winter through the

R.J. Phillips, *Rock and Roll Fantasy?: The Reality of Going from Garage Band to Superstardom*, SpringerBriefs in Business 35, DOI 10.1007/978-1-4614-5900-2_5,

Midwest, seems an ill-conceived idea on the face of it. Indeed, the poor planning and lack of adequate transportation led to the tragic death of three of the stars of the show in a plane crash.

5.1 The Winter Dance Party

Everything was wrong about the ill-fated Winter Dance Party. First, rock and roll was in a slump. Elvis was in the Army, Jerry Lee Lewis had married his 13-year-old second cousin and the resultant scandal nosedived his career, and Congress was getting concerned about payola among rock and roll radio stations. Though Alan Freed had helped pioneer the format for rock and roll shows of the 1950s, by 1959, the national economy was slowing down from the post-World War II boom, and rock and roll shows were trying to shore up profitability in a time of falling revenues. The only way to do this was to cut costs. One way the company that organized the Winter Dance Party, General Artists Corporation (GAC), cut costs was by contracting the tour buses with the lowest bidder in Chicago. Unfortunately, going with the lowest cost bidder is not always the best policy if standards are not upheld. The buses were not prepared for weather in winter in the Midwest where temperatures were sometimes 25° below zero during the tour.

Booking a rock and roll tour can be fairly complicated. There are some basic things that must be done by the booking firm. They have to find the venues, the means for the performers to reach those venues, and then collect the revenue and pay the performers. There was no national company such as Ticketmaster where fans could buy tickets and there was no Live Nation that owned and booked the venues. Rock and roll tours in the 1950s and 1960s played at local movie theaters, National Guard armories, or ballrooms. None of these venues were designed for amplified rock and roll.

The ballrooms were leftover from the Big Band days of the 1930s and 1940s. The site of the final performance of Buddy Holly, J.P. Richardson, and Ritchie Valens, the Surf Ballroom in Clear Lake, Iowa, had originally been built in 1933, burned down in 1947, and rebuilt in 1948. However, the instruments in the Big Bands were not amplified, though vocals might be, so that the acoustics of the ballrooms were not ideal for amplified sound. Though many of the songs were instrumentals, the Big Bands also often had a male or female singer. The Public Address (PA) system used was basically a vacuum tube amplifier and large microphones similar to what had been used in radio broadcasts. Monitor speakers so that the rock and roll musicians could better hear what they were playing were not used or were of a primitive design that did not enable musicians to hear all of the vocals and all of the other instruments. It was up to the drummer to keep the beat and keep the band together.

It is informative to map the Winter Dance Party tour through the February 2nd gig after which the plane crash occurred (see Fig. 5.1). The show had gone on for 11 consecutive nights culminating in the performance in Clear Lake, Iowa. Over the course of these 11 days, the Winter Dance Party troupe had traveled 2,665 miles. This is approximately the distance from Philadelphia to Los Angeles.

Fig. 5.1 The Winter Dance Party from January 23 to February 2, 1959 (Google Maps)

The Winter Dance Party tour began in Kenosha, Wisconsin (A), on January 23rd and was in Clear Lake, Iowa (G), on February 2, 1959. If they had booked the tour to minimize the distance traveled between the cities it would have been about 1,300 miles—one-half the distance actually traveled and an indication of the inefficiency of the tour dictated by the availability of the venues in those cities.

To get an idea of the inefficiency of tour travel in the 1950s, one can compare a typical road tour for a band today. Below is the 2000 tour route for the outlaw country band the Drive-By Truckers from Athens, GA (A), on April 4th and ending in Memphis, TN (O), on April 20th—15 gigs in 17 days and traveling 2,500 miles (Fig. 5.2).

The path of this tour is much closer to minimizing the total distance traveled. This is only possible when there are venues available on specified dates. Though some of this tour could have been by airplane, chances are that the band and the equipment traveled by bus a distance close to that traveled by the Winter Dance Party.

Why have tours generally become more efficient in minimizing distance traveled for bands? Undoubtedly improvements in communications are important, but it is also because the companies organizing the tours are better companies and oriented toward making profits and remaining in business for the long run. Indeed, GAC, which organized the Winter Dance Party, is still in business today, indicating that

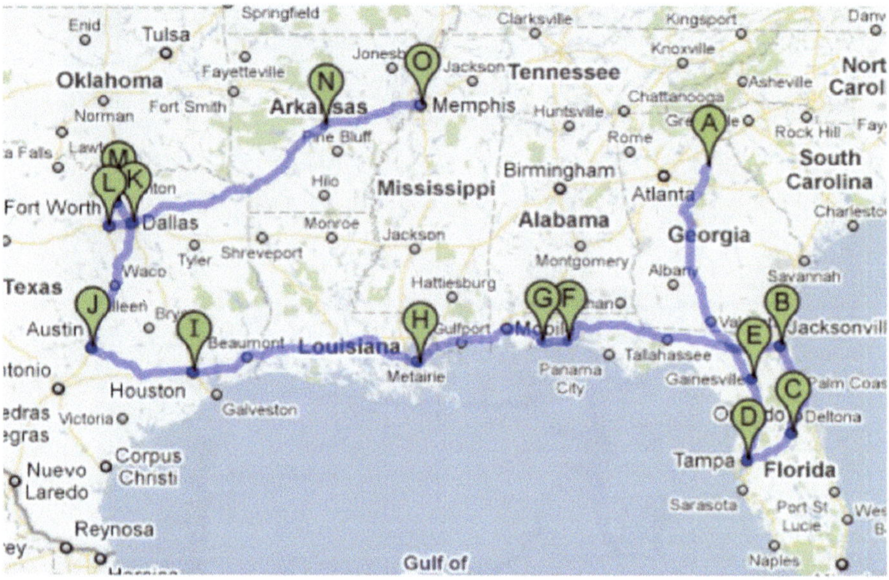

Fig. 5.2 Drive-By Truckers tour 2000 (Google Maps)

they have improved their business methods. The other reasons that tours are more efficient are that the means of transportation have changed and there is a greater availability of venues with desirable seating capacity and acoustics appropriate for amplified sound. The Drive-By Truckers tour was also able to travel the Interstate Highway system which was begun in 1956 under the Eisenhower Administration.

The Winter Dance Party was also not able to take advantage of the passenger railroad system either because the booking company was not able to coordinate the performance dates with the train schedule, or more likely passenger train service had been reduced by the late 1950s. In fact, for one segment of the Winter Dance Party, they were able to travel by train, though this was due to the problems with the buses. Nine of the eleven venues for the Winter Dance Party for this segment of the tour were ballrooms. At the peak of the system in the 1930s and 1940s, there were more than 27 different railroads operating out of Chicago in all directions. The Big Bands had a large number of members and the typical means of touring were by train. The band had had lots of equipment and lots of people. When the railroad network connected many small towns, then it could be profitable to tour which was important for the band members since it was their main source of income. Though Chicago was still the major hub for passenger rail travel (as it is today), by 1959, the passenger railway system had shrunk as bankruptcy and consolidation in the railroad industry led to fewer trains for small towns. The only option available for the Winter Dance Party was travel by chartered bus.

These two examples do not prove that all tours in the 1950s were inefficient and that all tours today are efficient in terms of minimizing distance traveled. Over a couple of decades, touring by Big Bands became more efficient and therefore more profitable. This was due to the booking agencies, the availability of ballrooms in smaller cities, and the widespread passenger train service in the USA. This system did not work for the rock and roll artists of the 1950s. Rock and roll tours were caught in a bind. There were no venues built specifically for rock and roll music and it was difficult to both book and travel to venues in smaller towns. This has changed dramatically today and enables groups at various levels of renown to be on the road profitably.

One of the keys to profitability in touring is ticket prices. For the performance at the Clear Lake, Iowa, on February 2, 1959, tickets were $1.25, and there were between 1,100 and 1,500 attendees. This means that the gross revenue was between $1,375 and $1,875 to split among the five acts—Buddy Holly (headliner), J.P. "The Big Bopper" Richardson, Ritchie Valens, Dion, and the Belmonts and Frankie Sardo. Tommy Allsup, Holly's lead guitar player on the tour, stated that he was paid $250 per week and bass player Waylon Jennings was paid $200 per week. Buddy Holly was paid $2,500 per week according to Allsup [98]. In 2009 prices, tickets were about $9 and gross revenue between $10,000 and $14,000 for one night while Holly, Allsup, and Jennings were paid $18,364, $1,836, and $1,469, respectively, per week. When you consider that there were performances every night and the tour lasted for over 3 weeks, it is pretty clear that touring was very profitable for the artists, venues, and GAC. Had he lived, Holly would have come home with nearly $60,000 in today's dollars, though this is low when compared with what comparable superstars earn today from touring.

As the demand for live rock and roll grew, so did the need for larger venues. Though today large-scale venues are common, it was the Beatles who were the first rock group to attract an audience to fill large-scale venues. It is not surprising that the first large-scale concert was held at a baseball stadium.

5.2 The Beatles at Shea Stadium

Playing every night of the week for 50 weeks is one way to sell a lot of tickets. However, life on the road can be grueling. "Touring can make you crazy, Ladies and Gentlemen." So begins Frank Zappa's movie, *200 Motels*, about life on the road for a rock musician. The venues that were available for bands in the 1950s and 1960s held 2,000 people if you were lucky. It is not until the arrival of The Beatles that there was sufficient demand to sell a larger number of tickets for one performance. The first large-scale rock concert was The Beatles 1965 concert at Shea Stadium in Queens, a borough of New York City. The Beatles were guaranteed $85,000 and a percentage of the receipts over $167,000. The ticket prices were $4.50, $5.00, and $5.75 and there were about 55,600 tickets sold. The Beatles share of the $304,000 gross was $160,000.

For their live performances, The Beatles were on stage for only 20–40 min. A series of photos taken at the 1966 concert at Shea Stadium shows that The Beatles took the stage a little after 9 pm and began performing 11 songs at 9:10 and left the stage at 9:50 a grand total of 40 min. Ticket prices were again $4.50, $5.00, and $5.75, but there were only 44,600 attendees. Assuming an average ticket price of $5.00, the gross revenue was around $223,000. In 2009 dollars, the ticket prices were around $33 and the gross revenue around $1.5 million.

When we look at large venue concerts today, the capacity and acoustics are light years beyond Shea Stadium where The Beatles had to rely on the Public Address system used to announce ball games for the vocals and their specially built Vox amplifiers for their instruments. No one could really hear them above the screaming of the crowd. In addition, because monitor speakers had not come into use, The Beatles were not even able to hear themselves. Stadiums are still in use throughout the world, but the Public Address systems are megawatts and with towers of speakers and instruments and vocals are put through the P.A. and soundmen at mixing boards assure that the sound is optimally adjusted for the venue.

The large venues that are built with music in mind generally hold about 20,000 people. But it is the sports stadiums with upgraded sound systems that have the greatest capacities. Giants Stadium in East Rutherford, NJ, holds 79,646 fans and was the top-grossing stadium in 2009 with 17 concerts. The Giants Stadium ranking at number one was a result of ten sellout concerts by Bruce Springsteen and the E Street Band which grossed $38 of the $51 million which placed the concerts at number one for the decade 2000–2009. The band U2 had the largest grossing tour in 2009 with 44 sellout concerts grossing $311 million and just over three million tickets sold. For the first decade of the twenty-first century, the largest grossing tour was The Rolling Stones with nearly $870 million gross and almost 8.5 million tickets sold. Though hypothetical, to provide some comparison with artists today, if Buddy Holly had toured 30 weeks per year, he would have had an income of around $600,000. That would be considerably less than what top artists like Bruce Springsteen, U2, and The Rollings Stones earn today for a comparable tour.

Whether large venues or small, all of the live performances discussed so far involve the band going to the fans. At least since medieval times when troubadours went from village to village to sing and entertain audiences, musicians have made their living primarily from this basic business model. The costs of traveling are borne largely by the performers. There is an alternative model that is exemplified by Las Vegas and Branson, Missouri—have the fans come to the band. When Bruce Springsteen plays for ten nights in a row at Giants Stadium and grosses $38 million, his travel costs are dramatically reduced. Playing every night in a different locale raises transportation costs and also wear and tear on the band members. Would Springsteen be better off playing for 2 weeks at Caesar's Palace in Las Vegas? Would fans, knowing well in advance that Springsteen was going to Las Vegas, be more likely to travel there than New Jersey?

5.3 Touring Costs

To get some idea of whether touring is better for bands, one can look at the costs of touring in Table 5.1. As an example, an article in *Forbes* published a representative breakdown of weekly touring costs for a band in 2003 for relatively large venues—5,000 seats.

Table 5.1 Typical touring expenses for a band playing 5,000-seat venues four to five times a week

Guarantees per week	$125,000
Management (15 %)	$18,750
Agency (10 %)	$12,500
Business manager (5 %)	$6,250
Band wages	$11,971
Crew wages	$14,934
Per diems	$4,130
Production costs	$9,750
Hotels	$7,722
Transportation	$13,840
Other tour expenses	$1,763
Equipment insurance	$2,500
Workers' compensation	$1,480
Total weekly expenses	$105,590
Net weekly income	$19,410

Source: [82]

The Colosseum at Caesars's Palace in Las Vegas seats 4,000 as does The Joint at the Hard Rock Hotel. The WAMU Theater at Madison Square Garden seats 5,600.

On a weekly gross of $125,000, the band's net income is <$20,000. Since most bands these days are organized as partnerships, this means that each member of a five-member group earns about $4,000. If the band tours 30 weeks out of the year, that is a respectable income of $120,000. However, if you were able to eliminate just the hotel and transportation expenses each week, that would double each member's weekly take home pay. The $120,000 per year becomes $240,000, or alternatively, the band only has to be on the road for 15 weeks a year—two-thirds of the year is not being on the road. This simple example shows how attractive it is for artists to have the fans come to them. In effect, those hotel and transportation costs are shifted to the consumers.

Of course, not all bands could sell out the Colosseum at Caesars's Palace, but it is not difficult to figure out what would be very lucrative—a rock and roll Branson, Missouri. If you had a concentration of 2,000 seat venues in an area, and booked bands from the 1960s, 1970s, and 1980s, everyone would probably be better off. The target fan group would be between the ages of 30 and 60 because they have the income to pay for the hotel and travel expenses. It might reduce the likelihood that grandma and grandpa will bring the grandkids to see Paul McCartney, but how many bands really have a multi-generation appeal?

5.4 Productivity in Live Performance

The costs of live performances have risen much faster than the overall level of inflation. The distinguished economist William Baumol has argued that the fine arts (music, art, and theater) suffer from a "cost disease" meaning that it is not possible to create live music in a "cheaper" way. The argument put forward is that there cannot be increases in productivity in performing a Beethoven symphony, for example, since the parts are written for all the instruments and they must be played identically over space and time. Baumol intended his analysis to primarily apply to the live performance of music rather than recorded music. Baumol, and his coauthor William Bowen, put forward the thesis that the arts suffered from this "cost disease" because of the inability to utilize technological change to increase the productivity of workers in the arts. Increases in productivity (more output per worker) are the key to increases in real income for workers and if productivity in the arts lags other sectors of the economy, then real incomes of artists will eventually fall relative to workers in other sectors. Does the "cost disease" help explain the rising costs of ticket prices at rock concerts? This is an important question because, in the future, live performance is likely to make up an increasing proportion of musicians incomes.

At first glance, the argument seems plausible because after all, how do you increase the productivity in song writing? If a performance of a song takes 2 min and 30 s, how do you increase the productivity of playing the song? However, as Tyler Cowen [38] points out, the cost disease would really apply more to a service such as men's haircuts at old-fashioned barbershops. The technology is fixed—razor and scissors—the skill of the worker is fixed—you can't give the same quality haircut in appreciably less time. This is a good example of an industry where productivity is stagnant and you expect declining income relative to other sectors of the economy. Not surprisingly, the old-fashioned barbershops for men where the barber uses a straight razor have been replaced by hair styling salons.

The Baumol–Bowen analysis of the cost disease problem does not take into account innovation in the arts, especially in rock and roll music. One way in which live music is more productive is that more people can hear the music either through larger venues or through recordings of the live performances. At rock concerts, though the fans like to hear their favorite songs from the band, they are rarely done in exactly the same manner—many songs are given extended length in live performance. Despite its initial appeal, the Baumol–Bowen cost disease problem does not seem to be one that should characterize modern music, especially rock and roll [38]. So if the cost disease does not account for higher ticket prices, what is the explanation?

5.5 Innovation in Live Music

Are ticket prices too high today? An examination of data from Pollstar on average ticket prices for 1,288 music concerts in 2009 gives a clearer view what is happening in the live music market.

Table 5.2 lists the top 20 acts ranked by average cost of ticket. Of the 20, 14 debuted in the 1960s or 1970s. Though some may have younger fans (McCartney for example), it would be expected that the audience is made up of those from the baby boom generation (born 1946–1960). Though he began his career in the 1970s, Vincente Fernandez, who was born in 1940, had his greatest success in the 1980s.

Table 5.2 Highest average ticket prices on Pollstar, 2009

Artist	Genre	Ticket price
Van Morrison	Pop/Rock	$173.89
Andrea Bocelli	Classical	$159.64
Cher	Pop/Rock	$140.56
Eagles	Pop/Rock	$132.15
Elton John	Pop/Rock	$126.04
Billy Joel	Pop/Rock	$125.61
Bette Midler	Pop/Rock	$123.42
Paul McCartney	Pop/Rock	$121.57
Eric Clapton	Pop/Rock	$116.69
Steve Winwood	Pop/Rock	$116.69
Celine Dion	Pop/Rock	$107.05
Leonard Cohen	Pop/Rock	$100.95
Fleetwood Mac	Pop/Rock	$96.34
U2	Pop/Rock	$93.77
Steely Dan	Pop/Rock	$93.61
Beyoncè	RB/Soul	$91.17
Vicente Fernandez	Latin	$90.87
Britney Spears	Pop/Rock	$88.04
Bruce Springsteen & The E Street Band	Pop/Rock	$87.86
Andr Rieu	Classical	$87.22

His appeal is also likely across generations. Andr Rieu, born in 1949, is a popular conductor and performer who leads the Johann Strauss Orchestra. Andrea Bocelli is an Italian singer who was successful singing opera and then crossed-over to the pop music market and he also may have fans of all ages.

This leaves only four acts that are contemporary rock superstars: U2, Beyoncè, Britney Spears, and Celine Dion. Though she began her career singing in French, Dion had success in the 1990s with English language recordings. Her greatest financial success began with her performances at The Colosseum at Caesar's Palace in Las Vegas beginning in 2002 and continuing to the present. The lavish production and higher ticket prices during this period have helped her sustain a touring career which commands top prices. Though her audience is likely more than baby boomers, she is not in the same category as the other two contemporary acts.

Britney Spears can be labeled a "teen pop phenomena" when she had her first number 1 hit in 1998 at the age of 17. Though her chart success has not been that great in the past decade, her regular appearance in tabloid magazines has enabled her to still command high ticket prices. It is highly unlikely that there are any baby boomers in her audience unless they are taking their grandchildren to the concert. Her future as a recording superstar is on the decline.

U2 emerged from Ireland in the 1980s and have had continual success since then. Their albums and tours rank them as superstars whose accomplishments have exceeded those of many artists from the 1960s. In terms of financial success, they will certainly exceed the financial success of The Rolling Stones—assuming Mick

Jagger and Keith Richards retire before they reach 80. A key part of U2's success is that they have continued to be innovative in their music and in their live performances. Their most recent—the 360 Tour—attempted to create a more intimate environment for their huge stadium shows. For the decade 2000–2009, their total touring gross of $844 million was second only to The Rolling Stones.

Beyoncè began her career with the female trio Destiny's Child who first charted in 1997. While still performing with the group, she released solo albums and has since become one of the biggest superstars in rock history. She won a record six Grammys in 2010. She is also a songwriter, producer, and actor. She is an innovative artist and has worked with a number of artists, including the top rap/hip-hop performer Jay-Z. Her career should last for many years.

5.6 Explaining High Ticket Prices

What is driving these higher ticket prices? Though increased costs as well as the popularity of an individual artist are factors, the rising incomes of the audience and the availability of larger venues enable these artists to charge these high prices. But do these high prices result in higher prices for other artists? Are aspiring performers being excluded from the market because they cannot command these higher prices? This question is difficult to answer without further data, but these prices have had an impact on touring.

One response to these high prices is the increasing number of music festivals. These festivals, for the most part in the summer months May to September, enable artists who have not had great commercial success to become known. Sometimes the festivals are topped by a well-known group, but many of the tours feature bands with only a regional following. For bands, they get national exposure, so they are willing to forego a huge financial gain from touring, and for the fans, they get exposure to a large number of new bands. What are the typical ticket prices for these festivals? Again from Pollstar.com we can see that the average ticket prices for festivals in 2009 were about $26 and range from $62.77 for the American Idol tour to $8.21 for the Sounds of Seattle Tour. The fact there are numerous bands at the festival brings down the cost per band and makes it a real bargain for the youth market. These festivals are really very similar to the tours of the 1950s, except that they are much better produced.

While the 2009 price of the Winter Dance Party tickets would have been $9 to see five charting artists, today that amount would only get you into a few festivals today. The increase in prices over this period of time, assuming the demand for music among teenagers has not appreciably changed, would be due to the increases in costs. However, the better sound systems, the better trained musicians, and the greater of efficiency of the tours also dramatically increase the quality of the musical experience. Though the baby boomers have to pay much higher prices today for the artists they wish to see, that is really driven by the higher incomes of the baby boomer generation.

5.7 The Ticketmaster/Live Nation Merger

Monopoly has always been prevalent in the music industry and it should not be a surprise that we find it in the area of touring. Presuming economies of scale in organizing tours, the rise of large national companies should not be a surprise. Recently there has been concern about the merger of the largest ticketing agency with the largest owner of venues in the USA. Given the history of artists' rebellion at Ticketmaster pricing, it is no surprise that *Billboard* titled an article about the Live Nation and Ticketmaster merger "Building the Perfect Beast." Live Nation owns the majority of amphitheaters in North America and promoted two of the world's top-grossing tours in 2009: U2 and Madonna. Ticketmaster's Front Line Management has relationships with more than 200 major touring acts, including the Eagles, Neil Diamond, Van Halen, and Christina Aguilera. The value of tickets sold through Ticketmaster was more than $8.9 billion in 2008 (*Billboard* February 6, 2010, p. 5). This merger ties the venues and the performers together and has the potential of providing the means for greater efficiency and innovation in offerings. In allowing the merger, the Department of Justice has sought measures to prevent monopoly power abuse in the tying of promoting and ticketing. If this merger results in creating greater value for the fans, then it can bring live performance to a new level. Though there is potential for monopoly abuse, this is tempered by the fact that live music performance is just one aspect of the entertainment industry. Today, there is such a wide range of possibilities—movies, television, and the Internet—that the possibility of one large company with monopoly exercising its market power is reduced.

5.8 The Future

One of the most important implications of the Internet and the digital revolution in music technology (MP3) is that musicians will once again have to make their living from live performance. The period when performers had the possibility of making a living from selling records lasted from the mid-1960s until the year 2000. Even during this period the vast majority of musicians made their living from live performances. It was only a small number of superstars like The Beatles or Michael Jackson who earned enough just from the sale of records. The Rolling Stones are one of the main groups that pioneered the model of earning vast sums from touring and playing songs from their large repertoire. The Rolling Stones never got really rich from the sale of records when compared with their post-1970 touring. The Rolling Stones had to earn their income from touring because it was not going to come from selling records. In the 1950s, tours were viewed as a way to sell records; in the future, recordings will be free or they will be sold in bundles with live tickets. Now that the revenue from recordings has fallen, it means that touring will be the main source of income. Whether these tours are live in-person appearances or on the Internet or a virtual world remains to be seen.

Chapter 6
Death: Elvis Has Just Left the Building

The mantra of "sex, drugs, and rock and roll" and the high profile deaths of a number of rock stars leads to the question of whether, in fact, rock stars are more likely to die young. A group of researchers in the U.K. found that indeed between 2 and 25 years from their initial rise to fame, rock stars tend to experience two to three times the risk of mortality expected in a similar group of non-rock stars matched by sex, age, and ethnicity. They note that a disproportionate number of the deaths are drug- or alcohol-related [12]. Though not covered in the study, when you add suicides and accidents, especially in planes and helicopters, it appears as though being a rock star is a risky business.

The death of a rock star, however, can provide another entrepreneurial opportunity for those who wish to keep generating revenue once an artist is deceased. Often times it is the immediate family who needs the source of income and they either take charge themselves or hire someone to aid in continuing the legacy and income of someone who may have died young through accident or suicide. For the typical person, at their death they have at most a house with a mortgage, savings including any retirement funds, and life insurance. What you have is the value of your assets minus your debt and that is your net wealth. It is not going to change after you "cash your chips." This is not true of rock stars who have built up an image and produced records and videos. It is quite possible for a rock star to be worth more after death. Though he had millions in debt, Michael Jackson's net wealth actually went up after he died. In November 2009, it was reported that reggae artist Bob Marley was likely to be the world's richest dead rock star by 2012. This and countless other similar stories raise the question of the impact of your demise on your continued success in the music industry.

6.1 The Day the Music Died?

In an earlier chapter I mentioned the death of the three stars of the Winter Dance Party—Buddy Holly, J.P. "The Big Bopper" Richardson, and Ritchie Valens. The case of Buddy Holly is of particular interest, though there have been efforts to make

R.J. Phillips, *Rock and Roll Fantasy?: The Reality of Going from Garage Band to Superstardom*, SpringerBriefs in Business 35, DOI 10.1007/978-1-4614-5900-2_6,

later generations aware of the contributions of "The Big Bopper" and Valens. When these artists died in 1959, the rock and roll era was just emerging as a popular musical style and its survival as a genre was not guaranteed. Holly's legacy in those first years after his death was pretty much left to Norman Petty, the producer who had created Holly's hits. Though he had written hit songs and sold a lot of records, after his death it was far from clear whether Buddy Holly would be remembered. His band, The Crickets, recruited Sonny Curtis and released an album in 1960 entitled "In Style with the Crickets." The album failed to chart, though ironically it contained a Curtis-written song that was destined to be one of the greatest rock and roll songs ever written and an anthem for all rock and roll musicians: "I Fought the Law."

Petty obtained demo tapes that Holly had recorded in his New York apartment in the months before his death. Petty took those tapes which had Holly singing and playing acoustic guitar and overdubbed them with full instrumentation using his studio band The Fireballs. Petty then released a "new" Buddy Holly album with these overdubs in 1963. The album called *Reminiscing* was on the charts for 17 weeks and peaked at number one.

Though Petty was criticized by some for doing this, in the 1990s, several long dead rock stars (including Buddy Holly and John Lennon) were able to release new recordings by the means Petty pioneered in the 1960s: old vocal tracks combined with new instrumentals. Natalie Cole recorded a duet with her long deceased father, Nat "King" Cole. The surviving Beatles recorded a "new" song with John Lennon that was packaged with the *Anthology* series.

In sorting out Holly's assets, which included the songs he had written, and his liabilities, Holly probably wasn't worth a lot when he died. What he lost when he died was his expected future earnings which could have been considerable. Holly had planned on building a recording studio to record himself and others. He hoped to reduce his live performances and make his living through song writing and producing others.

Holly might have faded into obscurity had it not been for his influence on the most important band of the entire rock and roll era: The Beatles. It also didn't hurt that the first U.S. single from the Rolling Stones was a cover of Holly's Bo Diddly-inspired "Not Fade Away." The release of the "The Buddy Holly Story" in 1978 sparked some renewed interest in Holly's recordings and a greatest hits album spent 12 weeks on the charts peaking at number 55. In 1996, a tribute album, titled *Not Fade Away: Remembering Buddy Holly*, was on the charts for 2 weeks peaking at 119. Rollercoaster Records in England continues to release obscure material from Holly's recording career. In 2011, there were three Holly tribute albums released.

Though Holly's songs are now being managed by McCartney Productions Limited, has the value of Holly's estate realized its full potential? In 2006, an obscure 1958 Holly-Petty penned song "Take Your Time" was used in a commercial for Visa. Reportedly, Visa paid over $300,000 for the license to use that music. Not bad for the use of 30 s of a song more than 50 years old. What does it take to continue to generate a revenue stream into the future for an artist who died at the age of 22 more than a half-century ago? Though Holly's songs are mostly under the control of McCartney's company, Holly's image is controlled by family members.

Holly's widow, Maria Elena Santiago, later remarried and divorced, but retained a strong interest in helping both keep Holly's name alive, and also in earning income for the Holly estate, which she controlled as his widow. No one could use the Buddy Holly name or image without her permission. It is not hard to imagine that she would not be looked on favorably either by Holly's family or in Holly's hometown of Lubbock, Texas. She was of Puerto Rican descent, lived in New York City, and was older than Holly. Years later, when the city of Lubbock decided that Buddy Holly's name could be a good way to promote tourism and economic development, they sought to use his name. Just prior to the fiftieth anniversary of Holly's death, Maria Elena reached a settlement where the city of Lubbock would pay her $10,000 a year for the next 20 years for the right to use Holly's name in a city monument to West Texas musicians.

Trying to keep a dead artist's memory around involves some basic economics. First of all, there must be a demand for the artist. Paul McCartney and The Beatles assured that future generations would know the name of Buddy Holly. But the basic problem is that there is a conflict between promoting the artist's memory and trying to maximize the value of the deceased star's estate. On the one hand, Maria Elena could let anyone use the Buddy Holly's name for free. It could be widely used, but this could tend to depreciate the value of Holly's image. On the other hand, she could be very restrictive and charge a high price for the use of Holly's name. How do you figure out how to make sure people remember Buddy Holly and at the same time maximize the revenue from selling the use of his name or image? It is not an easy problem to solve and is faced by any celebrity. Holly was one of the first rock and rollers to die tragically and he died at a time when the future of rock and roll was uncertain.

Though one can never know what these artists would have accomplished had they not died young, it is possible to get some idea by comparing them to similar artists and by examining the posthumous albums released. An obvious comparison to Buddy Holly would be Dion DeMucci who fronted the group Dion and the Belmonts on the ill-fated Winter Dance Party in 1959. Reportedly, Dion did not want to pay the $35 that the flight would cost him. The Belmonts had nine charting songs between 1958 and 1960 including the number 5 "A Teenager in Love" and the number 3 "Where or When." Dion left the group for a solo career in 1960 and a year later he had a number one hit with "Runaround Sue" followed by a number 2 hit "The Wanderer." Like many rock stars of the 1950s and early 1960s, the British invasion stalled Dion's career. Through 1989, Dion charted 23 songs, though his last big hit was in 1968 with "Abraham, Martin and John." Dion moved into recording Christian music in 1981. Dion was inducted into the Rock and Roll Hall of Fame in 1989.

Though the British invasion led by The Beatles had a negative effect on many performers, had Holly lived, it would have likely revived and strengthened his career because of his influence on groups like The Beatles and the Rolling Stones. It is even possible that The Beatles might very well have recorded at Holly's studio. The Buddy Holly legacy would be quite different from today had he not died young.

6.2 Can Death Be a Career Boost?

Contrast the uncertainty surrounding the value of Buddy Holly's estate after his death with that after the death of Michael Jackson. News that Michael Jackson made $72 million in the 4 months after his death raises the question whether or not your career, or at least your music, can continue after you die. Though many artists have died, there are only a handful of significant artists for which sales data is available from Nielsen SoundScan: Tupac Shakur, Michael Jackson, Kurt Cobain, George Harrison, Selena, and Notorious B.I.G. are examples. The most valuable assets for dead artists are the back catalogues of albums and single releases and any unreleased material. Live performances of dead artists seem to be in particularly high demand.

Let's first look at Michael Jackson. His biggest selling albums while he was alive were in order: *Dangerous*, *Thriller*, and *Number 1s*. However, his biggest seller after his death was *Number 1s*. The sales of the latter far exceeded its initial sales, but according to Nielsen SoundScan his biggest selling album while he was alive, *Dangerous*, sold less than 500 copies in the weeks immediately after his death. *Thriller*, one of his most widely known and critically lauded albums, ranked number two in sales after his death (see Fig. 6.1). The *This Is It* album quickly sold 1.5 million copies. In March 2010, a $250 million dollar record deal was signed for the Jackson estate—by far the largest recording deal ever, dead or alive. Are these business deals justified and will Michael Jackson's music continue to sell to future generations?

Though Jackson's music may continue to sell into the future, for other innovative artists it is less clear. Kurt Cobain was the leader of the group Nirvana and committed suicide in 1994. Cobain's life view can be summed up by noting that he reportedly wanted to call the band's second album: *I Hate Life and Want to Die*, but the record company talked him out of it [133, p. 346]. Cobain was distressed over the conflict between being an alternative, anti-establishment rock band that was commercially successful. Some equated commercial success with "selling-out" and therefore the music was no longer authentic. Nirvana had only released three albums at the time of Cobain's death in March 1994, though the first album released in 1989 was not widely available until it was re-released in 1992. An MTV *Unplugged* album released in late 1994 and an album of live recordings released in 1996 both went to number one on the *Billboard* Album Charts and stayed on the charts for 81 weeks.

The chart in Fig. 6.2 shows the sales of Nirvana's debut album from its release until late 2009. The release-to-date sales as of early 2010 were 4.7 million copies. An album, which sold nearly 170,000 copies the first week it was released and over 30,000 the week Cobain died, is also slowly fading away with very small annual peaks reflecting Christmas sales. Given the anti-commercial stance of Cobain and the band while he was alive, it seems as though their music may fade away, despite the influence of the band while Cobain was alive. However, the *Nevermind* album was re-released for the twentieth anniversary in 2011 with additional material. His widow, Courtney Love, has had various problems and was not able to sustain a music career for her own group, Hole.

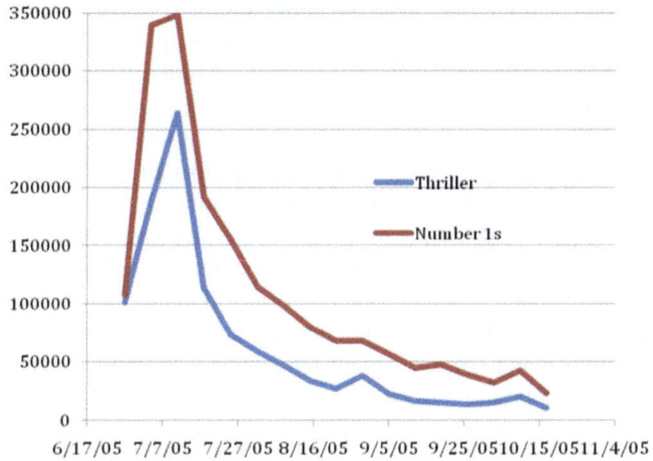

Fig. 6.1 Sales of Michael Jackson's *Thriller* and *Number 1s* following his death on June 25, 2009 (weekly). *Source*: Nielsen SoundScan

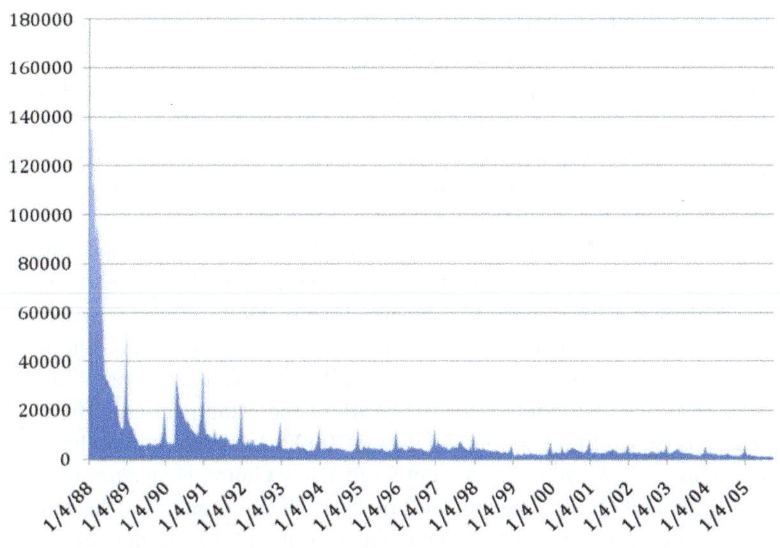

Fig. 6.2 Sales of Nirvana's debut album *Nevermind*. *Source*: Nielsen SoundScan

6.3 You're Nobody 'Til Somebody Kills You

Death also plays an important role in the early days of rap music. Though "gangsta" rap did not gain prominence until the mid-1990s, it came to represent to many people what was wrong with rap music. Songs like "Fuck the Police" by the Los Angeles group NWA were guaranteed to gain the attention of the authorities, and this likely added to the albums' sales. There was a huge backlash leading to Time Warner removing the song "Cop Killer" from the debut album of Body Count. There was a rivalry between rappers Marian "Suge" Knight and Sean "Puffy" Combs aka P. Diddy who traded insults and threats in their song lyrics. Conflict between the east coast rappers and the west coast rappers led to the arrests and deaths of a number of rap artists. This conflict came to a head with the deaths of Tupac Shakur in 1996 and Notorious B.I.G. in 1997. It seemed that in order to gain "street cred" and also bolster record sales, rap artists promulgated an outlaw image.

Prior to the first attempt on his life, Shakur had not had a number one album. After surviving one attempted murder in November 1994, his 1995 album, *Me Against the World*, went to number 1 on charts as did his follow-up album *All Eyes on Me* which was on the charts when he died. Three posthumously released albums also went to number one. To date, there have been 12 albums released since his death (Table 6.1). Though all but one went to number one, they didn't last long on the charts. However, the appearance of Tupac's hologram at the Cochella concert in California in 2012 may have helped increase the sales of his albums.

Notorious B.I.G. aka Biggie Smalls (real name Clarence Wallace) had a very short career. Only one album came out while he was alive, a second came out a month after died, followed by a third album of unreleased material, an album of duets, and a greatest hits album (Table 6.2). In 2009, a movie was released about the life of Notorious B.I.G. whose murder is still unsolved.

Figure 6.3 above gives sales for the week that marks the anniversary of Notorious B.I.G.'s death. On the third anniversary of his death, the album *Born Again* was released. Even despite the 2009 movie about his life and death, weekly sales of his albums are declining. However, his second album is the number one selling album by a dead artist with five million sold since its release.

Though both Tupac Shakur and Notorious B.I.G. are cited as influential early rappers, their recording careers do not offer much promise of continued commercial success. Other gangsta rappers like Snoop Doggy Dogg (Calvin Broadus) have since become more mainstream and become wealthy entrepreneurs. Snoop Dogg's 2009 album release *Malice in Wonderland* is still in the gangsta genre, but is devoid of the type of lyrics that would raise the wrath of the establishment. The change in Snoop Dogg is exemplified by the fact that in 2009 he rang the bell at the New York Stock Exchange. Ice T., who was a member of Body Count, is an actor on a popular TV show "Law and Order: Special Victims Unit." The commercial success of later rap stars provides some measure of what was lost due to the murders of Shakur and Notorious. Death was most certainly not a career boost for these artists who died too early in their careers.

6.4 How Do You Not Fade Away?

Neil Young once sang that it was better to burn out than fade away. The Beatles and Elvis Presley probably won't fade away anytime soon. Elvis is an industry and, like the movie idols Rudolph Valentino and James Dean, will always have fans among

Table 6.1 Albums by Tupac Shakur

Album	Entry position	Top rank	Weeks on chart	Entry date
2Pacalypse Now	77	13	34	2/1/92
Strictly for My Niggaz	4	4	67	3/6/93
Thug Life Vol. 1	6	6	65	10/29/94
Me Against the World	1	1	97	4/1/95
All Eyes on Me	68	1	105	2/24/96
The Don Kulluminati	58	1	103	11/16/96
R U Still Down	49	1	33	12/6/97
Greatest Hits	1	1	95	12/12/98
Still I Rise	2	2	28	1/8/00
Until the End of Time	1	1	1	4/14/01
Better Dayz	1	1	1	12/14/02
Resurrection	60	60	1	11/22/03
Loyal to the Game	1	1	1	1/1/05
Pacs Life	3	3	1	12/9/06

Source: Whitburn 2006a [151]

Table 6.2 Albums by Notorious B.I.G.

Album	Entry position	Top rank	Weeks on chart	Entry date
Ready to Die	3	3	88	10/1/94
Life After Death	25	1	90	4/5/97
Born Again	70	1	30	12/18/99
Duets: The Final Ch.	3	3	1	1/7/06
Greatest Hits	1	1	1	3/24/07

Source: Whitburn 2006a [151]

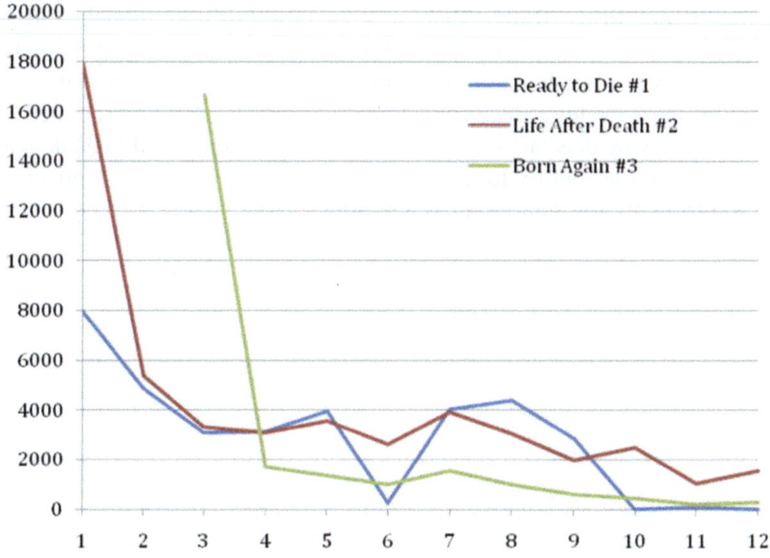

Fig. 6.3 Sales of Notorious B.I.G. albums 1–12 years after death in week of anniversary of his death on March 9, 1997. *Source*: Nielsen SoundScan

people born long after he died. The Beatles survived a breakup in 1970 and the death of two members of the band. Putting The Beatles on Rock Band and allowing the music to be remixed for a performance by Cirque du Soleil has kept revenue flowing for the surviving Beatles and the estates of the two deceased Beatles.

What do you do if you are not Elvis or The Beatles but rather Buddy Holly, Kurt Cobain, and Notorious B.I.G.? How do you continue to generate a revenue stream? The strategy that has been followed by the family of Jimi Hendrix is to release previously unreleased recordings. However, the problem is that no matter how many unreleased recordings there are of Hendrix performing, they are in fixed supply. The sale of CDs has declined, digital recordings are possible but generally less profitable, and the new business model for the recording industry is likely to be some sort of streaming that will further reduce the revenue from recordings. Ironically though, dead artists will likely fair better than live ones in selling digital recordings. One thing that is increasing is the use of songs in commercials, movies, and elsewhere. Is it possible that "Smells Like Teen Spirit" may one day show up in a deodorant commercial?

Are some artists worth more dead than alive? This could be the case if while they are living they are destroying their image and therefore economic value. Some might say that an overweight, drug-using Elvis Presley was destroying the image that he had built his career upon. If Elvis had lived, would he have reached the point that fans would be turned away from him? Elvis is a unique case, but certainly the administrators of his estate have done a very good job of continuing to earn income from his image and his music. Michael Jackson was having problems with his image as well. The various accusations and trials did not help his image. However, the strength of sales for his "This Is It" tour was strong.

The fact that the record companies are so focused on the sales of records by dead artists is also a statement about the state of the music industry from the perspective of the four major firms. Rather than seeking new business models and taking advantage of the enormous pool of new talent in the music industry, they are hoping to repackage "live" recordings of dead artists. It is hard to see how this is a good long-term business strategy since considerable resources must be expended in promoting recordings by dead artists. Furthermore, this strategy could be taken as further evidence that the century long business model that the record companies have utilized so profitably for themselves is nearing an end.

Chapter 7
The Technological Entrepreneurs: Engineers, Accountants, and Hippies

Technology made the recorded music industry possible, and despite current pronouncements of doom from record company executives, over the past century innovative entrepreneurs have always adapted technology so that more and more people have been able to enjoy music created by a growing pool of musicians [60]. As technology advanced, new musical styles were created when musicians were able to interact with different musical genres. In turn, the musicians influenced the technology that was created. Leo Fender, who could not play or tune a guitar, would never have created his path-breaking Telecaster guitar had there not been a demand for such an instrument. New technologies brought lower cost means of producing recorded music, but, at the same time, threatened the distribution of music by older methods. The recorded music industry significantly decreased the demand for sheet music, much as the later rise of cassette tapes and CDs decreased the demand for earlier technologies. Technological invention and musical style innovation have gone hand-in-hand since the nineteenth century.

Writing in 1906, at the beginning of the era of recorded music, the greater composer and performer John Philip Sousa wrote:

> I foresee a marked deterioration in American music and musical taste, an interruption in the musical development of the country, and a host of other injuries to music in its artistic manifestations, by virtue—or rather by vice—of the multiplication of the various music reproducing machines.

Sousa believed that people would listen to recorded music and therefore have less interest in developing their own musical skill. People would lose interest in live performance and instead be content with listening to what Sousa called "canned music." Artists now have an array of technologies that on the surface would appear to improve the quality of music. Auto-Tune is one such technology that basically enables anyone to sing on key (or out of key, if you wish). Not everyone gets to be a rock and roll star, but today with games like Rock Band and Guitar Hero just about anyone can satisfy the desire to be a rock star for at least the length of the time of a song. Today people can be musical without any musical knowledge or training. One wonders what John Philip Sousa would say

R.J. Phillips, *Rock and Roll Fantasy?: The Reality of Going from Garage Band to Superstardom*, SpringerBriefs in Business 35, DOI 10.1007/978-1-4614-5900-2_7,

about this development. Do we lament the decline in the ability to play the piano, or celebrate the fact that more people can enjoy making music electronically? In his attack on the "menace of mechanical music," Sousa made two fundamental points. First, the mechanical reproduction of sound would become a substitute virtually everywhere for live music and society would suffer as the overall musical development of the country declined. Second, the composers of the music were not compensated for the music they created. What Sousa could not have foreseen is that at some point the cost of distributing recorded music would fall and this would in turn increase the demand for live music. Some thought that radio would decrease the demand for live music. But if recorded music is free, then consumers can spend their income elsewhere and increasingly that is on live performances.

The movie "Blackboard Jungle" is often credited with starting the Rock and Roll Era because of its use in the opening credits of the 1954 release "Rock Around the Clock" by Bill Hailey and the Comets. The three songs used in the movie provide a capsule depiction of the evolution of musical style and technology from the 1920s to 1950s. In one scene, the teacher attempts to use his collection of 78-rpm jazz records to help teach mathematics to his students. However, the students are not really moved by his playing of early jazz great Bix Beiderbecke's performance of "Jazz Me Blues"—a recording dating from 1924. They ask if the teacher has anything by Frank Sinatra or Joni James. After perusing through the teacher's valued collection of old 78s, a student asks "Does anyone want to hear Cherokee?"—a song written and recorded by Ray Noble in 1938. He tosses the record across the room shattering it and then tosses the box of records into the air. The old 78s were so fragile that record companies automatically deducted a 10% loss due to breakage for the records produced—thus reducing the total number on which they had to pay artists' royalties. Incidentally, this breakage deduction stayed in contracts until around 2000, even though the problem of breakage largely ceased with the advent of vinyl records.

Using the same phonograph, a student then puts on Stan Kenton's "Invention for Guitar and Trumpet" recorded in 1952. In reality, this song would have been played on the new technology of long-playing 10 in. albums at 33 1/3 rpm. Ironically, the rock and roll song, "Rock Around the Clock" was originally released as a 78 rpm on Brunswick in 1954 and had only modest chart success. However, after the movie was released, the song was re-released on the main Decca label as a 45 rpm. Brunswick, which as noted earlier, released The Crickets' "That'll Be the Day," became Decca's "rock and roll label subsidiary."

In this chapter, I will focus on the entrepreneurs who created recorded sound, those who created the electric guitar, and those who improved the quality of amplified live music. Without these inventions, and subsequent innovations, it is inconceivable that we would have had Elvis, The Beatles, or Public Enemy. The stories of the inventions and innovations are often complex and filled with lawsuits and intrigue. In this story, what is clear is that there are a number of important characteristics. What is crucial is interaction between the musicians who create music and those who are creating the technology to produce the music.

7.1 Recorded Sound: Thomas A. Edison

For most of history, musicians had to rely upon live performances. Cowen ([39], p. 132) notes, as a commodity, early music was neither durable nor reproducible: there were no musical scores and no way to record the music. By the time of Mozart and the other classical composers, the sale of sheet music was a supplement to income from live performance. The possibility of recorded sound began with the invention of the phonograph by Thomas Alva Edison in 1877. This first phonograph was not an electrical machine but acoustic. Speaking into a horn while turning a crank resulted in marks on a tin foil cylinder that could then be replayed. Edison obtained a patent for a recording machine in 1878 and founded the Edison Speaking Phonograph Company the same year. Edison's representatives traveled the world in 1878 and 1879 to demonstrate his "wonderful speaking-machines." Visitors to these shows were allowed to speak some words into the funnel, which would then be replayed by the machine [142, p. 15]. An improvement to the original Edison phonograph was made by Chichester Bell (cousin of Alexander Graham Bell) and Charles Sumner Tainter, who substituted a layer of wax for the tinfoil covering the cylinder and improved the design of the stylus [142, p. 4]. They called their improvement the graphophone and a long period of lawsuits ensued that was not settled until the early twentieth century.

Edison thought that the phonograph would replace stenographers. For this reason, the diaphragm and reproducer for the Edison machines would reproduce a voice talking in a regular tone, but the early Edison machines did not provide high quality for singing or musical accompaniment. In 1888, Gianni Bettini, a member of the landed gentry in Italy and a cavalry officer living in the U.S., acquired an Edison phonograph and wanted to use it for recording music. He redesigned the diaphragms and reproducers so that they would provide a higher quality recording. Bettini had neither electrical nor mechanical training, but simply in taking apart the phonograph determined how he could improve it [118, p. 70]. Bettini and his wife were quite popular in social circles in New York, and many stars of the Metropolitan Opera were recorded with his machine.

One of the Edison Home Phonographs, with the improved Bettini diaphragm and reproducer, was also acquired by Lionel Mapleson, who was the librarian for the Metropolitan Opera. Edison later gave another model of his phonograph to Mapleson and both were used in recording the New York opera. Many of his recordings made between 1901 and 1904 at the Met are still in existence and are considered today to be valuable recordings of the opera in this time period. Mapleson has been labeled the "father of bootlegging." However, as the record industry began to develop in the early twentieth century and more recordings were made for sale to the public, Mapleson was no longer able to make his bootlegs. Opera singers began to record for Columbia and Victor as a source of income. The recognition that the sale of recordings could be an important source of income for a performer led to the development of a phonograph that could play prerecorded cylinders and later discs.

7.2 Prerecorded Music: Louis Glass

The father of the modern record industry was Louis Glass, the chairman of the Pacific Phonograph Company, who added a coin-in-the-slot mechanism and four headphone pairs to the dictation machines and set them up at the Royal Saloon in San Francisco in the late 1890s. For a nickel per play, patrons could hear the sounds of a prerecorded entertainment cylinder [142, p. 6]. Others soon followed this business model of essentially renting prerecorded music and the music boxes appeared in saloons, amusement parks, and retail shops across the U.S.

The company that became very successful at this "coin-in-the-slot" business was the Columbia Phonograph Company, which had been established originally by Jesse Lippincott who had been involved in trying to promote business adoption of the phonograph but his company failed. In 1888, entrepreneur Lippincott had purchased the distribution rights for the graphophone and the patent rights to Edison's improved phonograph [142, p. 6]. Since 1890, Columbia had focused on music production and made improvements to the graphophone, including a redesign that enabled it to play Edison cylinders which led to yet another round of patent lawsuits with Edison that lasted until 1896 [142, p. 7].

Edison formed a new company in the same year, the National Phonograph Company, and began to focus production on the coin-in-the-slot music boxes. While all of this was going on, another inventor, Emile Berliner, a textile merchant who conducted chemical and physical experiments and was an immigrant to the U.S., began to study the Phonautograph that had been invented by Leon Scott in 1857. In 1887, Berliner applied for a patent on a sound recording instrument under the brand name "Gramophone." It used a technique to record sound with a needle on a medium turning horizontally. He began to experiment and found a method to etch rather than engrave the sound grooves in the medium. Though the response to his Gramophone was not particularly positive, he continued working on his invention. He later invented a method of pressing a negative of a metal plate that he had first etched as a positive and thus could begin pressing hard-rubber plates. At the time, for the cylinder recordings, it was necessary to use ten recording devices to produce ten copies of one recording session. With Berliner's method, one could now reproduce the recording and mass production was possible, though his interest lay in making music recordings and copying them, not in the mass production of Gramophones for entertainment for the public [142, p. 10].

Berliner returned to Germany and, with the help of others, established Deutsche Grammophone in 1899. Another wave of patent lawsuits occurred in the U.S. involving new entrants into the market and the Victor Talking Machine Company that was founded in 1901. Though Edison continued to make cylinders, the flat disc record established itself as the standard by 1902 and the lawsuits had come to an end with an agreement between the Victor Talking Machine Company and the Graphophone-Columbia group on the mutual use of the record patent rights. This is considered the beginning of the modern record industry as we know it—at least until the changes of the digital revolution in the past decade [142, pp. 14–15].

The important difference is that it established a medium for playback, but not recording. Consumers were sold a copy of a recording that they could use for their own home listening enjoyment or could pay to listen to coin-in-the-slot machine music.

In 1948, Columbia records introduced the 12-in. vinylite long-playing (LP) record onto the U.S. market. LPs played at 33 rpm and were much better in sound quality, durability, and price. RCA had also introduced the 45 rpm record which was superior to the 78s, but the length of the music that could be put on a 45 was much less than the LP. Together with the developments in tape recording, the costs of entering the recording industry were greatly reduced [141, p. 118]. Thus in the 1950s, both the 33 rpm and 45 rpm records thrived because the 45 rpm records could be issued with a potential hit single on one side and a "B-side" that was intended as a bonus for buying the hit record. If the single was a hit, then an album could be produced.

In the years preceding the invention of recorded sound, who were those most opposed to recorded sound in the music industry? It was the sheet music companies that proliferated in Tin Pan Alley in New York City. As Tschumck notes, once profits began to increase for the phonographic industry, the publishing companies' revenues were threatened. Though musicians had long wanted a copyright law for music, it was only when the publishing companies' profits were threatened that they began to lobby Congress for copyright laws which were enacted in the Copyright Act of 1909. The Act stipulated a fee of 2 cents for each music cylinder, record, and piano-roll—something lobbied for by John Philip Sousa, who was one of the most successful recording stars of the period. This law laid the foundation for the establishment of the American Society of Composers, Authors, and Publishers (ASCAP) to begin collecting those royalties in 1914 [142, p. 35]. This law united the interests of Tin Pan Alley with those of the phonographic industry.

7.3 Multitrack Recording: Les Paul

As Strobl and Tucker ([132], p. 114) note, the rise of popular music on a global basis is a post-World War II phenomenon. Despite the inventions of the radio and the phonograph, record sales remained low in the first half of the twentieth century. Phonographs were expensive to purchase and maintain, and the quality of the 78 rpm records was not very good—they were thick, heavy, the sound quality was not good, and they were easily broken or scratched.

As the phonograph industry shifted from selling machines to the consumers for their own recordings, and instead became focused on selling prerecorded music, there remained the problem of recording the original sound. Today, with the aid of computers, an almost unlimited number of tracks can be recorded for a single song. The method of recording for the early cylinders and disks was quite primitive from the present-day perspective. The performers would gather around the horn and play. There was no possibility of balancing the sound of the trumpets from the sound of the violins other than adjusting the placement of the musicians from the phonograph. Once the shellac disks and cylinders could be mass produced from a master recording, there was only the need for one recording. However, there was still only one track and no way to balance the instruments. The development of radio and especially the microphone improved the quality of recorded sound. This led to the creation of an electrical recording machine with a diamond needle that could cut into acetate to create a master and from that master records could be mass produced.

The next great breakthrough in recording was the invention of multitrack recording. Though with all innovations, many may have tried to do this, it was one man, Les Paul, who is considered the father of multitracking. Les Paul, who died in 2009, has long been recognized as a guitar innovator and the person who designed the Les Paul guitar for the Gibson company. However, Les Paul's achievements in recording perhaps surpass his success as a recording artist. In 1930, Les Paul became the first known person to record a multi-instrumental performance. Because magnetic recording tape did not exist, he did this by building up guitar tracks on an acetate disc [44, p. 25]. Though Les Paul took the idea of multitracking to record companies, they were not interested in the possibilities it afforded for the recording artist. This technology of multitracking using an acetate disc was used in a few recordings in the 1930s. Patti Page used the technology in her 1947 recording of "Confess." The record was marketed as being performed by "Patti Page and Patti Page." She also used the technology in her next release, "With My Eyes Open, I'm Dreaming" to create four-part harmony.

Though developed by AEG/Telefunken in 1937, magnetic recording tape machines were not widely used in the 1940s. During World War II, the Germans had developed magnetic tape recording and used it for their propaganda radio broadcasts. When the tape recorders were brought back to the U.S. after the war, companies began to develop their own models. One of the first was made by Ampex. The future of music recording was changed forever when Bing Crosby gave one of the early Ampex machines to Les Paul as a gift. The quality of the tape recorded sound was superior to that of the acetate disc.

Unlike the acetate method, the tape recorder was above all mobile. Les Paul also realized that by adding a fourth recording head to the Ampex machine, sound-on-sound would be possible. By spacing the heads on the Ampex, Paul was able to achieve a tape delay, another important recording innovation. The use of these techniques is what enabled Les Paul to produce the innovative music he recorded with Mary Ford in the early 1950s. Their recording "How High the Moon" was number one for 9 weeks in the spring of 1951. By 1954, Ampex and others had introduced stereophonic reel-to-reel tape recorders with sound-on-sound capabilities.

This was not the end of the recording innovations introduced by Les Paul. He created a device he called the "Les Paulverizer" which attached to his guitar and enabled him to record and play back numerous guitar parts live on stage. It was also Les Paul who suggested to his friend David Seville the possibility of recording at different speeds and The Chipmunks's recordings were born. As the Rock and Roll Era began, Les Paul worked with Gibson to create a solid-body guitar that rivaled those designed by Leo Fender in terms of desirability; the early models still command top dollar in the vintage guitar market.

The recording industry was also helped by the surplus of audio equipment left over from World War II, especially high-quality microphones. This enabled the creation of numerous recording studios throughout the U.S. Two of the most important were the Sun Studios in Memphis run by Sam Phillips and the Norman Petty Studio in Clovis, New Mexico. Phillips recorded on acetate discs at 78 rpm and then made an acetate master on his Presto 60-N lathe and turntable [44, p. 36]. He also had a Presto five-input mixer that accommodated four microphone inputs. In 1951, Phillips began using magnetic tape and eventually purchased a Presto 900-P recorder which would allow recording at either 7 or 15 in./s. Elvis Presley was the biggest artist to record for the Sun Records label, but cash flow problems coupled with a high demand for Presley recordings led Phillips, as noted earlier, to sell his contract with Presley to RCA in November 1955.

7.4 The Low-Cost Recording Studio: Norman Petty

The invention of magnetic recording tape created the possibility of low cost recording studios. In the creation of a recording master on a diamond-cutting machine that etched the master recording in acetate, a mistake in performing would require the creation of a new master. Recording tape allowed re-recording at a lower cost—merely erase and re-record. After World War II ended, much of the military's recording equipment was sold off at bargain prices [44, p. 3]. The independent recording studios began to flourish. Using the techniques pioneered by Les Paul, Petty was able to make overdubbed recordings [44, p. 43]. In addition to Buddy Holly, Petty produced hits for a number of artists including Buddy Knox's "Party Doll."

Petty was one of the first to really use the recording studio as an instrument in creating music. For example, when recording Holly, Petty not only would place a couple of microphones on the amplifier to record the sound, but also place a microphone near the guitar strings to pick up the sound of the guitar pick as Holly played. Petty also utilized the technique of overdubbing that Les Paul had taken to great heights in his recordings. Though Petty in the 1950s did not have a multitrack tape recorder, his Ampex 600 could be used both in and out of the studio and an Ampex 327 mono machine on which he could make duplicate copies. He would use the two machines to overdub and then mix the recordings.

To avoid sound bleeding from one instrument to another, Petty had the musicians placed in different rooms. Also, with the help of Buddy Holly's family who was in the tile business, Petty and Holly created a tiled room away from the main recording studio in which to record vocals with a natural echo effect. Petty used a wide selection of very high-quality microphones made by Telefunken, RCA, and Electrovoice and placed them in spots that would enhance the sound of the recording by miking the snare drums and kick drums. The main control room contained Altec 604 monitor speakers and an elaborate mixer. In designing his studio, Petty was influenced by the acoustic properties of the recording studios in New York, so the walls of his studio were not flat, but contoured. Though there would later be disputes over money and songwriting credits, there is no doubt that Petty made an enormous contribution to the sound and success of Buddy Holly and the Crickets.

Though Petty continued to record artists, both groups and solo artist, he never repeated the success he had with Holly. Petty's greatest post-Holly success was probably when he put The Fireballs together with Jimmy Gilmer in the early 1960s. The band produced a string of regional and national hits including "Sugar Shack," "Daisy Petal Picking," and "Bottle of Wine." "Sugar Shack" was the number one *Billboard* song for 1963 and "Bottle of Wine" was a cover of Tom Paxton's folk version that remains one of the classic songs of all time. The Fireballs still perform today with original members Stan Lark, and innovative lead guitarist, George Tomsco.

7.5 The Electric Guitar: Adolph Rickenbacher, George Beauchamp, and Leo Fender

There is a disagreement on who "invented" the electric guitar. Many individuals were working on this because there was clearly a demand for an amplified guitar so that it could be heard with a Big Band orchestra. The technology of the microphone was well known in the twentieth century, but there remained the problem of producing a high-quality sound reproduction without feedback. Though "Rock Around the Clock" marks the beginning of rock and roll, the instruments used by Haley's band were an accordian/piano, standup bass, saxophone, drums, steel guitar, and Haley played a hollow-body electric guitar. On recordings, the lead guitar riffs were played by studio musicians and on stage by either Haley or the steel guitar. Though not the first to create an electric guitar, one man essentially created the instruments of rock and roll: Leo Fender. He created a guitar whose basic design is still in production today, and the vintage guitars created by Fender in the early 1950s are prized collectors items owned mostly by wealthy enthusiasts, including musicians like Bruce Springsteen and Eric Clapton.

The story of the electric guitar begins with the innovation in musical style found in Hawaii in the late nineteenth century. Instead of playing and fretting the guitar in the normal manner, the instrument was laid flat and an object such as a glass bottle was run over the strings. Hawaiian music became popular in the U.S. in the mid-1920s and so did the electric steel guitar. George Beauchamp, a vaudeville performer, violinist, and steel guitar player, asked John Dopyera, a violin repairman, to produce a guitar that used the nonelectric phonograph technology and had a Victrola horn attached to the bottom. This instrument was not satisfactory, but Beauchamp took the reproduction head off the Victrola which had a small mica disc attached to a needle and when the needle vibrated while playing a record, the disc mechanically amplified the sound through the horn [129]. This led to the creation of the Dobro, a guitar that had aluminum resonators to amplify the sound. This was not an electric guitar, but it was amplification based on Edison's original acoustic recording phonograph.

By 1930, it was well known that magnetically sensitive metal moving through a magnetic field caused a sound disturbance which was translated into an electrical current when a coil of wire was placed adjacent to it. This was the key to a guitar pickup. After experimenting with a microphone attached to the top of a hollow-body guitar,

Beauchamp then attached a Brunswick electric phonograph pickup to the one guitar string test board. In place of the phonograph needle, he ran a metal guitar string. The problem Beauchamp realized was that he needed a way to translate a guitar string's vibration into an electrical signal [129, p. 9]. Beauchamp's experiments eventually led to what is considered the first electric guitar which was nicknamed the Frying Pan or Pancake guitar. The pickup was two horseshoe-shaped magnets and one coil of wire. He filed a patent on June 2, 1934 that was granted on August 10, 1937.

Beauchamp formed a company with Adolph Rickenbacher and others to produce electric steel guitars made of Bakelite—one of the first plastic compounds that was used to make many products, including bowling balls. The Electro String Instrument Company continued to produce steel guitars and eventually the company's name was changed to Rickenbacker—using a k instead of h for easy pronunciation of the German name. The Rickenbacker company was successful with its Hawaiian steel guitars and its electrified hollow-body Spanish guitars. The creation of the solid-body electric guitar was created by another whose name would become synonymous with rock guitars.

Leo Fender was not trained as an engineer and had 2 years of accounting at a junior college. He had some musical training on the piano and saxophone, but he liked the sound of stringed instruments. According to his long-time friend and business partner, Forrest White, Leo especially liked Hawaiian music. Graduating from high school in 1928, Leo built and rented Public Address (PA) systems from 1930 to 1947. In 1938, he opened Fender's Radio Service in Fullerton, California. He soon thereafter met Doc Kauffman, who had worked with George Beauchamp, and the two formed K and F Manufacturing Company. In 1943, they designed a new pickup with the guitar strings passing through the magnetic pickups magnet wire coil instead of under the coil as with other pickups. They were granted a patent on this new pickup on December 7, 1948. In 1945, they built the first six K and F lap model Hawaiian steel guitars along with a newly designed amplifier. However, the two soon ended their partnership and Leo changed the name of the business to Fender Electric Instrument Company.

Paul Bigsby built a solid-body guitar for the country artist Merle Travis in July 1947, and its design influenced Leo Fender. It was in 1950 that Fender first built his single pickup solid-body guitar called the Esquire and a two-pickup version called the Broadcaster. Because the guitar company Gretsch had been marketing a drum set with the name Broadkaster (with a k), the name of the two-pickup version was changed to Telecaster. According to Leo, the name was used because television was just becoming popular at the time. The guitar body design of the Telecaster and Esquire remains today one of the most recognized in the world and the Telecaster is still in production. But the Telecaster was not to be the last of Leo's innovations in solid-body guitars.

Though the Rickenbacker company produced an electric bass guitar in the 1940s, it had no frets and was played in the same manner as the standup bass. Fender produced the first electric bass guitar with frets in 1951 and called it the Precision Bass. In addition to guitars, Fender also began to produce amplifiers which were covered with a tweed material.

Fender had already achieved great innovations in guitar making, but it was with the assistance and advice of Bill Carson, the lead guitar for Hank Thompson's band, that Fender created the quintessential rock guitar: the Stratocaster. The innovations on this guitar included six separate sections for the bridge, the back of the guitar had a contoured body, and the jack receptacle was at a 45° angle. Fender added his own design of a tremolo bar, though both George Beauchamp and Paul Bigsby had already created tremolos. Prototypes of the guitar were made in 1954. This guitar has been utilized by many great guitarists including Buddy Holly, Dick Dale, Eric Clapton, and Jimi Hendrix. Bob Dylan had been a teenager when he saw Buddy Holly on the Winter Dance Party Tour playing a Stratocaster, and years later, when Dylan famously "went electric," he chose a similar sun-burst Stratocaster. Each of these guitarists were great innovators in musical style, and the Stratocaster was a crucial element in their playing. Guitarists quickly utilized a trick to change the sound of the Stratocaster by positioning the three position pickup switch between two of the settings. This threw the pickups "out of phase" and in the hands of Jimi Hendrix helped create the "psychedelic" sound. Later Stratocasters incorporated a five-position switch to create the same effect.

Fender was very successful and was incorporated in 1959. In 1964, the company was sold to Columbia Records Distribution Corporation (CBS) for $13 million. Unfortunately, the quality of Fender guitars went down dramatically and collectors of vintage guitars always make the distinction that the most prized instruments are "pre-CBS." Leo Fender resigned from the company he had founded. In addition, his contract with CBS placed constraints on his ability to start a new company. Together with other former Fender employees, a new company was founded in the early 1970s called Music Man, but was sold in 1984 and the company ceased production under the Music Man name. In 1985, Bill Schultz and associates purchased Fender from CBS, and since that time, the quality and reputation of Fender guitars and amplifiers has been restored.

7.6 Live Sound: Bill Hanley and Mike Matthews

In the final "Tonight Show with Conan O'Brien," Will Ferrell led the Tonight Show Band in a rendition of the Lynyrd Skynyrd classic "Freebird." Featured on lead guitar was Billy Gibbons of ZZ Top. Gibbons was playing through a circa-1965 Silvertone amplifier that was originally sold through the Sears catalogue. When I was in junior high and high school, we only dreamed of one day owning a Sears Silvertone amplifier. They were highly regarded then, and as evidenced by its use by Gibbons, they are still prized amplifiers. Why is this the case? The vacuum tube technology utilized in the Sears Silvertone amp is over 100 years old!

The answer lies in the difference to the human ear between digital (pure) sound and analog. The fact is that most guitar players prefer the "warmer" sound of vacuum tube amplifiers. Vacuum tubes enabled the amplification of sound waves and thus permitted the guitar to be heard at a level not previously available. It was no surprise that other instruments like trumpets, clarinets, and saxophones were prominent in the Big Bands of the 1930s. However, the amplifier meant that the guitar could now take center stage. One characteristic of vacuum tube technology is that even though it enables amplification of the sound wave, it does so with some distortion. The designers of vacuum tube amplifiers sought to minimize this distortion. Ironically, it is this remaining distortion which makes the vacuum tube technology desirable today. Though transistor technology became available in the 1960s, they were initially less reliable than the vacuum technology and this impeded their adoption. Today, vacuum tube amplifiers from the 1960s are very desirable, while those made with transistors are not in demand. Amplifiers today use both old and new technology by incorporating the tube technology into the preamp and digital components to power the sound without the need for the very weighty and heat producing transformers of earlier tube amplifiers. In the heyday of tube technology radios, RCA was a leading producer of vacuum tubes. Where are vacuum tubes made today? Russia.

With the collapse of the Soviet Union and the beginning of the transition to a market economy in 1990, there was great upheaval in the countries of the former USSR. Industries that had been state-owned and provided with subsidies from the government were now faced with global competition. The result was a steep rise in unemployment as inefficient state-run enterprises collapsed. However, in the midst of this transition, there was a bright spot, ironically due to the technological lag of the former Soviet republics. For more than 60 years, vacuum tube technology was utilized in televisions and radios in the U.S., but by the late 1960s, transistors replaced vacuum tube technology in most modern western economies such as the U.S. However, this was not true in the communist countries. Vacuum-tube technology, which had a long history and was very reliable, was still used in many applications. In the western countries, the only use of vacuum tubes after the 1970s was in either guitar amplifiers or very expensive amplifiers for audiophiles. Since RCA, Westinghouse, and others that had produced vacuum tubes for televisions and radios no longer produced them, the only source of vacuum-tubes was the state-run companies. The leading company in this area was Sovtek—which had a virtual monopoly on the world supply of vacuum tubes when the Soviet Union collapsed. So what happened to the company?

Enter Mike Matthews, an inventor and entrepreneur whose company Electro-Harmonix produced effects pedals for guitar players. In 1998, Mathews purchased the ExpoPul factory in Saratov, Russia which produces two thirds of the world's vacuum tubes. ExpoPul was a state-owned enterprise that began production of vacuum tubes in 1953. The brand name for these vacuum tubes was Sovtek. Despite a 2006 effort by shady businesses in Russia who sought to put him out of business, the factory continues producing vacuum tubes under the Reflector Corporation name. Mathews, through his company Sensor Corporation, also owns the rights to the Sovtek trade name in the U.S.

7.7 Testing, Testing, One Two Three: Neil Young

Another innovation in the 1960s was the use of monitor speakers to enable performers on stage to hear what they were playing and singing. Normally, a Public Address (or P.A.) system has speakers that project the music out to the listeners. The members of the band each had amplifiers and the drums were presumed to be loud enough on their own to not need amplification. The early P.A. systems for rock and roll bands were little more than amplifiers that had been used for public speaking in large rooms. The amplifiers and the microphones were not made for the high volumes that characterized rock and roll music. The vocals would need to be very loud to be heard over the amplified guitars. The arrangement of having speakers in front of the performers meant that they could not hear themselves playing. This, of course, made the drummer very important because everyone would key off the drummer who was expected to keep the beat. There's a good reason why orchestras have a conductor—how else would all of the musicians be able to stay together during the performance because they cannot hear the other performers.

In the late 1960s, however, someone figured out that you could place speakers to face the performers so that they could then hear themselves sing and therefore do a much better job of live performance. Once monitor speakers came into general use, the musicians could both stay in tune and in time with each other much better. One has to only listen to the recordings made of The Beatles at the Hollywood Bowl or Shea Stadium to realize just how impossible the situation was during their performance. They had huge guitar amplifiers and a powerful P.A. system, but no monitor speakers. The fans could not hear them because of the screaming, and the band could not hear themselves playing at all.

The first use of in-front monitors speakers is attributed to Neil Young, when he was with Buffalo Springfield, and had enlisted Bill Hanley as the sound consultant. Interestingly, one of the first opportunities to apply the monitor speaker system was at the 1969 Woodstock Music and Arts Festival. One can even compare the live recordings of the same bands that played at the Monterey Music Festival in 1967 with the 1969 Woodstock performances to see the difference monitor speakers make. Musicians can actually hear themselves play. Hanley was the person who did the sound at the Woodstock Festival in 1969. The fact that the Woodstock album was the first successful, high-quality live album is testament to the technological accomplishments of the Woodstock hippies.

As the P.A. systems were improved and the amplification and number of inputs increased, the drums and later the instruments were all miked through the P.A. system. Thus, one can compare the Crickets, who played with one guitar amplifier, a small drum set, a cheap low amp P.A. system, and a stand up acoustic bass, with the setup that contemporary bands have available. The P.A. system today may have a 100 inputs with several microphones on the drums alone. Indeed, monitor speakers themselves have been replaced with small earphones that enable the musician to hear everything that is coming from the stage. There is no doubt that technology has greatly improved the quality, and therefore, the productivity of rock and roll music.

7.8 Technology and the Future of Music

There is a sense in which the phonograph as it developed in the twentieth century was similar to the facsimile or fax machine technology. With the fax machine, you could send an image over space electronically, but the end user does not have an electronic image. The scanner and email are substitutes for the fax machine which now seems to be an obsolete technology. What we have now is the technology for the consumer to record and duplicate electronic recordings, and this can be seen as a direct descendent of Edison's original phonograph.

There is a real sense in which the digital and computer revolution have brought home music back to the possibilities of Edison's phonograph. An entire recorded music industry was created using a technology that is now obsolete. The recording/playback technology developed as two distinct technological evolution and business models, but today both recording and playback have been transformed by the digital revolution and the Internet. Consumers can now download digitally encoded recordings and, using the same equipment, can also make their own recordings.

Personal computers and available software have driven down the costs of recording. A quick read of album liner notes shows that this technology is being used extensively in many recordings. Apple provides a program called "Garage Band" with all of its computers that lets you record directly into an Apple computer with amplifier settings that capture the major vintage amplifier sounds. It contains numerous prerecorded loops and instrument recordings and allows you to produce professional quality recordings for $50 [94, pp. 51–53].

As technology progresses, there will be innovators and entrepreneurs who will expand the possibilities of music. Though perhaps a shock to John Philip Sousa, the electronic era has opened the possibilities of music performance to more people and created a society where music continues to be performed at home and songwriting and live music remain vibrant. The Digital Age offers the possibility of the realization of Sousa's dream that everyone be able to create music. There is a bright future for music in the Internet Age, but not necessarily for companies that try to operate with an outmoded business model. For a relatively brief period in the twentieth century, record companies made profits by selling prerecorded music. They will not be able to do that in the same way in the twenty-first century.

Chapter 8
Absolutely Free: Only If You Want It to Be!

Is digital technology coupled with the Internet destroying the music industry as we have known it since the turn of the twentieth century? Yes. Is that necessarily a bad thing? No. So how will the record companies stay in business? They won't, if they try to maintain the same business model into the future. That model was to earn revenue from the intellectual property rights attached to recorded music. The record company's response to declining sales was to go after those who were illegally downloading copyrighted digital recordings. The record companies instead got lots of bad publicity. In 2004, Apple launched a campaign with Pepsi to give away 100 million free downloads and used people who were sued by The Recording Industry Association of America (RIAA) in the commercial promoting iTunes. Who will consumers have a more favorable view of? [26]. Even as the record companies realized that going after illegal downloading was a road with many pitfalls, technology has made downloading illegally passè. Who really wants 80 gigs of music stored on their computer? What music lovers want is to be able to listen to all of your music whenever and wherever you want. Mobile devices such as the iPhone, Blackberrys, and the iPad make this possible. It should be no surprise that just as the music industry is beginning to come to terms with the problem of illegal downloading, a new technology is making it increasingly irrelevant. Record cylinders took up space, 78s took up storage space as did 33 rpm and 45 rpm records. MP3s also take up storage space. Streaming music services allow you access to your songs on any computer or mobile device.

The record companies are now gearing up to fight free streaming of music because the revenues from streaming are even less than from downloading. All of this indicates that recorded music will someday be absolutely free, but that does not mean that musicians will no longer be able to make a living by performing music. Instead, as has always been the case in the past, innovation and new business models will assure an increased supply of music and a means of making a living doing it.

R.J. Phillips, *Rock and Roll Fantasy?: The Reality of Going from Garage Band to Superstardom*, SpringerBriefs in Business 35, DOI 10.1007/978-1-4614-5900-2_8,

8.1 Jimi Hendrix and Jerry Garcia Lead the Music Industry into the Twenty-First Century

Jimi Hendrix died in 1970 at the age of 27 and Jerry Garcia died in 1995 at the age of 53. Ironically, they provided the means for a successful business model in the recorded music industry in the twenty-first century. How can this be? Their successes after their deaths are due to the fact that both died with lots of unreleased recordings.

On May 8, 1970, I attended a Jimi Hendrix concert in the gymnasium on the campus of the University of Oklahoma in Norman. Performing with him that night were Billy Cox on drums and Mitch Mitchell on bass guitar. They opened the set with "Fire" followed by "Spanish Castle Magic," "Machine Gun," "Lover Man," "Foxy Lady," "Hear My Train," "Message to Love," "Red House," "The Star Spangled Banner," "Purple Haze" and closed with "Voodoo Child (Slight Return)." How can I be sure about all of this? After all, this was 40 years ago in an era when a distinct aroma often permeated the audience as "funny" cigarettes were passed among the crowd. I found the information on the Internet.

This was a momentous time in the U.S. It was only 4 days after four students at Kent State University in Ohio had been shot by the National Guard during an anti-Vietnam war demonstration. Hendrix was wearing a black armband that said "KS4." This armband had been made by antiwar students at OU and many in the crowd were also wearing the armbands. Suppose I could buy a copy of that concert. How much would I be willing to pay for it? Today, as a relatively affluent baby boomer, I might be willing to pay $100 or more for that recording. Since the recording was not available, I went to iTunes and downloaded live performances of Hendrix during roughly the same time period and put them in the order of the concert I attended. I can listen to that concert anytime I wish on my iPad or iPhone. Jimi Hendrix had the foresight to record many of his live performances and also left unreleased studio recordings. This is what will enable the Hendrix estate to earn income for a number of years into the future.

But what if I had been a "Deadhead" in early 1970 and attended a Valentine's Day concert by the Grateful Dead at the Fillmore East in New York City? I can buy an MP3 version of the concerts played on February 13th and 14th for $15.99 on iTunes. The recordings were made on a two-track machine and the quality is not the best, but do I care? What did it cost to produce this live, unmixed album? Close to nothing. How much did The Grateful Dead earn from that recording from 1970 until its release on CD in 1996? Nothing. What have they earned since its release on iTunes? Only Apple and the surviving members of the band or their descendents know for sure. In retrospect, it looks like the Grateful Dead brilliantly planned for continuing a revenue stream after most of them were really dead. One could go further and say that the Grateful Dead developed a futuristic twenty-first century business model for earning income from prerecorded music. In addition to iTunes, Wolfgang's Vault—recordings made at the venues of legendary promoter Bill Graham—are also making available both free and subscription recordings of live performances. The requirement for earning revenue from this business model is that you, in fact, be dead and cannot make any more recordings. This is the dilemma the recorded music industry faces for the future.

As the cost of creating and distributing recorded music declines, the market price will tend to zero. Who would like for this price to be zero? Certainly not the record companies, but what about Apple? What would happen to the demand for its various mobile devices if recorded music were free? They would sell many more millions throughout the world. As Apple's revenues go up, the record companies see their revenues decline. In fact, when Apple agreed to try a three-tier pricing strategy for its music—69 cents for older music, 99 cents for recordings encoded with Digital Rights Management (DRM), and $1.29 for DRM-free recordings, *Billboard* reported that revenues for the record companies actually fell. In 2010, Apple purchased the streaming music service Lala.com which provides streaming versions of licensed songs for 10 cents and lets you upload your music library to be available anywhere. In 2011, Apple released iCloud which enables the streaming of your entire musical library to all devices. This is why the record industry today is afraid of Apple and afraid of the future.

8.2 The Current State of the Music Industry

There are different explanations for the decline in music sales that began in the 1980s. Some authors suggest that the decline was predominantly related to poor quality of the recordings—cassette tapes were notably poor in sound quality. There was also a global recession during that period which had a potential impact on sales that was not solely related to the cassette. It is also possible that a shortage of creative work contributed to the decline. The popularity of Disco music in the late 1970s faded and was replaced with superstars like Michael Jackson, whose album *Thriller* was released in late 1982. Though MTV had begun in 1981, it did not play videos by black artists in the beginning [88, p. 11].

Though it is unrealistic to assume that double-digit growth rates in CDs shipped could continue for long, the enormous drop in the growth rates is unlikely to be explained solely by macroeconomic conditions. During the period 1990–2002, world economic growth fluctuated as well, but there appears to be little correlation between CDs shipped and economic growth. Thus, the explanation must be in other factors. The two primary suspects would be the development of substitutes to music entertainment (movies, computer games, satellite TV and radio, etc.) and the availability of bootleg or pirated music.

As Strobl and Tucker [132] discuss, improved technology and the superior sound quality of CDs increased the demand for music beginning in the 1980s. The music quality was better because of recording improvements and the expanded use of digital formats. Sales indicated that consumers were willing to pay more for higher quality recordings. In the early to mid-1990s, sales of CDs were increasing at dramatic rates. Sales of CDs grew at an astonishing rate of nearly 35% in 1994. By 1995, CD sales comprised 60% of the units sold and 70% of the market value of sales [132, p. 115]. With the expanded use of the Internet and file sharing, participants began to realize that they were able to obtain free music off the Internet. Shopping on the Internet for CDs and DVDs also lessoned the importance and role of the record store. Record stores' share of total market sales fell from 56% of the market in 1993 to about 39% in 2002. On February 9, 2004, the venerable Tower Records indicated that it was filing for bankruptcy, citing declining sales from Internet piracy and from prices being undercut from Best Buy or Wal-Mart.

With the development of technology and file sharing advances by 2001, the International Federation of the Phonographic Industry (IFPI) estimated almost 40% of all CDs and cassettes sold in the world were pirated copies. Global sales of pirate CDs have more than doubled in the past 3 years and now generate an illegal international business worth US$4.6 billion, according to IFPI. The industry experienced negative growth approaching 10% in sales of CDs in 2002. Global sales of recorded music were down over 50% from 2000 to 2008 and have generally continued that trend to the present. Digital sales have shown a modest increase since 2011.

During the CD boom of 1984–1999, Steve Knopper states that the big music companies made three serious mistakes that affected the subsequent development in the industry and intensified the problem with illegal downloads [88]. First, was the use of the "long box" to package CDs. It was a huge waste of resources and did not appear to be environmentally friendly. Second, as documented by Fredric Dannen in *Hit Men* [46], record labels began to use independent radio promotion as a means to increase sales. NBC Nightly News responded with a series on "The New Payola." Finally, in opposing the use of Digital Audio Tape (DAT), the record companies went along with allowing computer companies such as Apple to include built-in recording devices without paying royalties to the record labels [88, pp. 70–78]. The latter resulted in an increase in ripping and burning CDs. The record companies during this time also eliminated the single record format, and consumers were forced to buy albums only. All of these things, combined with the creation of the MP3 format, were to lead to the problems of the music companies after 1999. The digital revolution also helped create the rap and hip-hop genres that relied heavily on sampling. Though possible with recorded tape, digital editing made the process easier and more precise. By 2000, the major music companies and some artists began to raise concerns about the future of the music industry.

In the past, new technologies brought lower cost means of producing recorded music, but at the same time, threatened the distribution of music by older methods. The recorded music industry significantly decreased the demand for sheet music. There is little doubt that the major music companies' aggressive pursuit of those who illegally downloaded music also raised the implicit cost of downloading music from the Internet. Apple discovered that there are lots of law-abiding citizens who want cheap music. Far from the Internet threatening the end of music, it really only threatened the status quo in the music industry.

Like the invention of recording tape and Compact Discs, the Internet is more likely to ultimately result in a very large increase in demand for music once the new business models are in place. The challenge for the music industry is to figure out a way to get consumers to pay for the music they download. The iTunes Music Store by Apple has apparently been successful in this regard. If downloading is cheap and easy, then consumers will not be willing to spend the time and face the possible litigation connected with downloading for free from Napster-type web sites.

In the current environment, the dissemination of pirated copies of music may promote an increase in demand for live performances. It is thus possible that a decline in the demand for legal recordings, coupled with an increase in demand for illegal recordings, could lead to a change in how those in the music industry earn their revenues. The Rolling Stones have not had a hit song in two decades, but they are among the highest grossing musical acts and, as noted in an earlier chapter, at least two thirds of their income is from touring.

The industry has progressed, however, from the days of organ grinders and those who would stand up in crowds and spontaneously sing songs for compensation in hopes of gaining a greater audience for the music. Today there are two fundamental choices for the distribution of the music. One is to rely upon the record distributing companies and the radio network, and the second is the Internet. The crucial difference between these two distributions networks is that the former is dominated by monopoly, while the latter is pretty much free competition.

8.3 Is Capitalism Destroying the Music Industry?

Economists have long had a problem with explaining how a capitalist or market system operates in the real world and how they correspond to the views of the average person about how capitalism works. In textbook capitalism, everybody seeks their own self-interest, and with minimal government involvement, everyone is better off. Adam Smith invoked the "invisible hand" as the explanation for the harmony of self-interest and societal interest. The problem is that what most people think of as capitalism is a world where they try to make as much money as possible by restricting or eliminating competition. In the economists' pure world of free market capitalism, contracts shouldn't exist. Contracts bind you to an employer when instead you could be free to work for one employer 1 day and another employer the next day. This is the way pure capitalism would work, but of course no one wants it. As we saw in an earlier chapter, contracts introduce what economists call transaction costs—contracts must be monitored, for example—and they significantly alter market outcomes. The world of free, perfect competition is a myth, but a powerful one.

In a capitalist economy the entrepreneur receives a huge monetary reward by creating something that consumers want and no one else is producing. In creating something new, the entrepreneur creates a temporary monopoly. How long does the monopoly last? Until someone else creates a similar product at a lower cost. In a *laissez faire* world, any government involvement that would protect the entrepreneur's monopoly profits is bad. Patents and copyrights are just such protection. This "game" of government protection has gone on for a very long time. However, people have come to accept this view of capitalism that patents and copyrights are necessary to enable the capitalist economy to operate. Exactly the opposite is the truth.

8.4 Why Copyright?

Those who innovate and create something new (entrepreneurs) are able to appropriate longer revenue streams or what economists would call above "normal" profits—the opportunity costs of the entrepreneur. As other competitors enter the business and provide competition, those above normal profits are competed away. The industry expands, prices fall, and society is made better off. However, the issue of copyrighting or patenting modifies this basic analysis. The argument for patents or copyrights is that the innovator must be assured of above normal profits for a length of time to ensure that the costs of creating the new product are recouped. It is argued that failure to do so would decrease the amount of innovation in the future. The question is whether public policy should intervene to lengthen the time period for continued above normal profits [5, 41, 143].

The beneficial impact of copyrights and patents on consumers is questionable. In a recent study, Waldfogel could find no evidence that illegal downloading affected the quantity of new, acclaimed recorded music or new artists coming to the market [145]. For example, consider the implications of stopping the illegal production of music CDs or DVDs in Southeast Asia. Given the high costs of producing legal products, but the relatively low costs of producing illegal products, would society be better off if illegal copying were prohibited totally? It should be obvious that it does not imply that legal copies would then be purchased. The issue is the relative price of legal vs. illegal goods. The music companies seek to prohibit illegal activity which further raises their costs of producing legal products. A solution to the problem would be to lower the price of legal products. Such a strategy would likely shift the demand from illegal to legal products.

The development of file sharing on the Internet has become the most significant concern of firms in the recording industry. The industry believes that piracy is its Achilles heel. The industry typically assumes that piracy and legitimate recordings are perfect substitutes. This is not in fact the case. Indeed, it may be—as the groups The Grateful Dead and Phish discovered—that there can be a positive impact on the demand for legitimate recordings from the increase in supply of pirated recordings. It is difficult to assess the true impact of piracy given all of the rhetoric. However, some believe that the music industry may have vastly overestimated the losses due to piracy. According to a study by Hui and Png [77], the impact of piracy on the music industry was much less than estimated by the industry—about 42% less. Hui and Png estimate the losses at 6.6% of sales. However, because piracy helped keep prices down, in the absence of piracy, the music companies could have charged higher prices and generated larger revenues.

It is not until the invention of the player piano and the phonograph that courts begin to confront the issue of copyright in music [154, p. 364], [74]. An 1897 Amendment to the original Copyright Act established that copyright owners had the sole right to regulate public performances of their copyrighted songs [155, p. 365]. In 1908, the Supreme Court ruled on the issue of the copyright of music in a case involving the mechanical reproduction of sound by a player piano. When the White-Smith Music

Company discovered that their tunes were being used on a player piano, they filed for copyright infringement. "Player pianos" produced music by an operator rolling the perforated sheets over ducts connected to the mechanical parts of the piano and atmospheric pressure forced sound and created the melody of a song. The Supreme Court ruled that since the player piano was not a "copy," no violation occurred. Congress responded with the Copyright Act of 1909 [155, pp. 364–365].

Copyright law was passed by Congress in 1909 to protect the vested interests of the sheet music publishers. Congress was also concerned about monopoly in the mechanical reproduction of songs (Edison Records and others), and therefore awarded the copyright owner the exclusive control over mechanical reproduction and royalties. The copyright owner, as noted, would be the songwriter and the publishing company unless the songwriter had sold his rights to the publishing company. The Edison Company could not reproduce the music on cylinder or flat record without the payment of a fee–labeled "mechanical royalties"—to the copyright holder [123, pp. 37–38]. Copyright owners could not prevent reproductions of their work, but they were entitled to royalty payments for each reproduction [155, p. 365]. The Harry Fox Agency, founded in 1927 by the National Music Publisher's Association, is the foremost mechanical licensing, collections, and distribution agency for U.S. music publishers. From 1909 to December 31, 1977, the statutory mechanical royalty rate was 2 cents for all songs. Presently, it is 9.1 cents for songs 5 min or 1.75 cents per minute or fraction thereof for songs over 5 min [146].

Radio was also becoming popular in the early part of the twentieth century and was of concern to the publishing companies. In 1912, songwriters and publishers created the American Society of Composers, Authors, and Publishers (ASCAP) to license performance rights to broadcasting outlets, primarily radio at this time [123, p. 44]. Radio was required to pay performance royalties to the copyright holder—the songwriters and publishers [155, p. 364]. Radio was not required to pay performance royalties to the performing artists and labels because it was argued that playing records on the radio would lead to record sales and mechanical royalties payable to the artists and labels. This royalty payment scheme continues to the present-day, though, as will be discussed below, it is under attack by artists and labels represented by the RIAA.

In 1941, an association of radio stations set up a rival licensing organization to represent those who had been ignored by ASCAP. Thus, Broadcast Music Incorporated (BMI) represented hillbilly, race, ethnic, and foreign artists [67, p. 5]. In the 1950s, it was BMI that represented the emerging rock and roll artists. ASCAP did not view the competition favorably, and it was ASCAP, among others, that urged Congress to actively pursue "payola" in the music industry in the late 1950s. The Society of European Stage Authors & Composers (SESAC) was founded in 1930 as a performance rights society for European and gospel music. Soundexchange was founded in 1995 as a performance rights group that collects and distributes royalties from digital performances of music. All of the performance rights groups must collect information from the various media that use music and then calculate how much each copyright owner should receive.

Though the PROs reveal the basic structure of how compensation is paid to songwriters, it is far from transparent and is subject to great error. There is no reason to believe that they would intentionally pay artists less than they deserved. What the PROs first do is sell licenses for music used by a variety of outlets from major television stations to your local bar. This generates a certain level of revenue. Then by sampling which songs are actually played, the PROs determine the relative importance of the song in the market and in principle the performance royalties are paid on that basis. There are adjustments made for how the music is featured (movie theme, background music for example), where it is performed, how much the licensee pays the PRO, and the time of day. Each song earns credits, there is a value to the credit determined by the total revenue taken in each quarter, and the performance royalties paid are simply credits earned times credit value. Figure 8.1 depicts the role of ASCAP in collecting and distributing performance royalties.

A fundamental problem with this system is that it is one where there is no real competition between the PROs to lower prices charged for the collection of this information [51]. They may offer slightly different services, but the argument is that the collection of the data is so complex and represents such a huge cost that the industry is effectively run as a shared monopoly. As a songwriter, you do not have the option to collect the information on your song independently because it is too expensive for you to monitor every possible user. It is a "take it or leave it" proposition from the PROs. This monopoly model has recently been questioned by some [83, 84]. An additional confusion has arisen with the various bills introduced in Congress to force terrestrial radio stations to pay performance royalties to the artists and record companies. Since the beginning of recorded music, the artists and record companies have received mechanical royalties on the sale of their recordings, and not performance royalties. Of course, with the rise of the Digital Age and the Internet, these mechanical royalties, which come from a mechanical license issued by the Harry Fox Agency primarily, have fallen dramatically. This is why record companies are near bankruptcy and artists have taken to the road to perform live to earn income.

There are companies that have created new business models for music publishing which promise to undermine the industry as it has existed for a century. The problem with the copyrighting of songs that began apparent in the early decades of rock and roll is that many songwriters lost control over their compositions—John Fogerty of Creedance Clearwater Revival being a prime example. How do you avoid this situation? The answer is to have a contract between the artist and the music publishing company whereby the songwriter explicitly does not give up copyright control. This is the model of Kobalt Music that promises the artists greater, fairer, and more timely compensation without Kobalt Music owning the copyright. Obviously, in the short-run this is a less profitable business operation than the old system, but that is because the latter was based on monopoly power of the publishing company. A more competitive system, made possible by developments in technology (tracking songs, and so on), is one that will work better for artists and still enable companies such as Kobalt to be profitable because more artists would sign up for such a contract [1, 33].

Fig. 8.1 Structure of ASCAP royalty distribution

8.5 Brother, Can You Spare a Dime?

How much are you willing to pay for a song? For all of the music industry's concern that the Internet and the Napster-model of providing free music would lead to the collapse of the industry, Apple's iTunes Music Store has demonstrated that consumers will pay for music downloads on the Internet. Consider the downloading of music from Napster. As originally structured, it drove the price of a song down to zero. Thus, anyone trying to provide an identical product would face a difficult time trying to make a profit. How could you survive under such a cost structure? Steve Jobs and Apple computer, through the establishment of the iTunes Music Store, provided that new business model.

In a survey of university students, Gallaway and Kinnear found that consumers were willing to wait a short time to acquire the music legally before exchanging MP3 files and there was a substantial willingness to pay for a legal MP3 file. These two groups represent separate markets because people have self-identified with respect to their preferences regarding legal/illegal behavior. Those who are willing to wait to download music legally will not enter the market for illegal music. This assumes that the market can be divided into two groups with differing demand curves for the good or service. Everyone is familiar with the fact that consumers are often charged different prices for consuming the same good. A simple illustration is peak and off-peak pricing for bus, metro, or airfares. In her 1933 work, *The Economics of Imperfect Competition*, the economist Joan Robinson analyzed this price discrimination by firms [120].

Regarding the question of illegal downloads, Gallaway and Kinnear conclude:

> This suggests new technologies are not only good for consumers but also compatible with profits. By recognizing the varying elasticities of demand for music of various ages, an intertemporal price discrimination model may secure requisite profits, promote efficiency, and encourage consumers to engage in ethical behavior. This business model would allow firms to profit and instrumental technology to flourish [63, p. 286].

Had the music industry heeded early evidence in this regard, they may have avoided the bad publicity associated with their prosecution of illegal downloaders [31]. Price matters, and cheaper MP3s, and the unbundling of music in an album format could have countered the negative impact of Napster and similar peer-to-peer systems.

8.6 The End of the Winner-Take-All Market?

In a market economy, people are supposed to be paid according to how much they contribute to producing the output of goods and services. Sports and entertainment are often cited as examples of "winner-take-all markets." The primary characteristic of these markets is that they are dominated by a few outstanding individuals who garner very high wages, while the rest of the people working in the field earn comparatively modest salaries [59]. In baseball, Alex Rodriguez earns millions in annual salary, while the non-superstar earns a salary in the low six figures. Not bad, but there is great dispersion in salary differentials. In areas where careers are often short because of age and physical limitations or popularity of a musical style, it can be difficult for the average non-superstar to sustain a level of income that exceeds alternative employment [66]. The superstars in these markets have a degree of monopoly in the selling of their labor services. It is exploitation in reverse—it is now the capitalist who is exploited, but there is also a negative impact on other workers.

In their book *The Winner-Take-All Society,* Robert Frank and Philip Cook sought to explain why in entertainment and sports it is generally the case that there are a few very highly paid superstars at the top, and a very large group of lowly paid players and entertainers at the bottom [59]. Can it be the case that talent is so unequally distributed in society, or are there other possible explanations? According to Frank and Cook, the winner-take-all markets can arise whenever pay is determined by relative rather than (or in addition to) absolute performance [59, p. 24]. The outcome is not necessarily desirable, since in a society where winner-take-all markets are prevalent, the unequal distribution of income has a depressing effect on economic growth, according to Frank and Cook. The reason is that the competition in these markets leads to a misallocation of resources in society. Those at the top earn more than they would in competitive markets based on absolute performance. Of course, in entertainment and sports where large amounts of public funds are often used to build venues for these performances, there is an additional cost to the consumers of entertainment and sports.

Frank and Cook argue that the solution to the problem of winner-take-all markets is to place limits on the wasteful competition. Doing so will improve the allocation of resources and presumably increase economic growth. This conclusion is not necessarily one that everyone would support. However, the crucial point made by Frank and Cook is that the markets are not competitive free markets in the first place. Indeed, there is a failure of the market system to allocate resources to their highest valued use and therefore intervention through government regulatory policy is appropriate.

Consider now the impact of the winner-take-all market in rock and roll music. The Rolling Stones earn millions from their concerts and recording sales. They are able to advertise and direct the consumers to their music in ways that small bands just starting out cannot. This does not mean that the Rolling Stones are an evil monopolist trying to keep consumers from enjoying other performers, it is rather a consequence of the establishment of their brand name and the industrial organization of the industry. If tickets to a Rolling Stones concert are $200 and consumers allocate a fixed budget for concerts, then there is less money available to spend on other performers.

Applying the Frank and Cook solution would require limits on the salaries paid to rock and roll superstars. The large entertainment companies would love to have these limits, but the public policy issue would be to make sure that the above normal income that was taken away from the superstars is not just transferred to the entertainment companies, but rather directly benefits the consumers and society. The regulation of markets is not an easy task, but it is one that is necessary in modern society. Hopefully, the costs of regulation do not exceed the costs of the market failure or society is no better off.

The other possibility for dealing with winner-take-all markets is the development of technology. The creation of the Internet has led to a potential for reducing the costs of disseminating information about musical groups. Though it does not make the playing field totally level, fundamentally both the Rolling Stones and the local rock band have access to the Internet. In this case, technology increases competition and helps to eliminate the institutional structures (the record companies, radio, and so on) that helped create the winner-take-all market. When a few superstores negotiate contracts with a few record companies, it is not surprising that compensation is higher. The record companies believe that they can still profit on

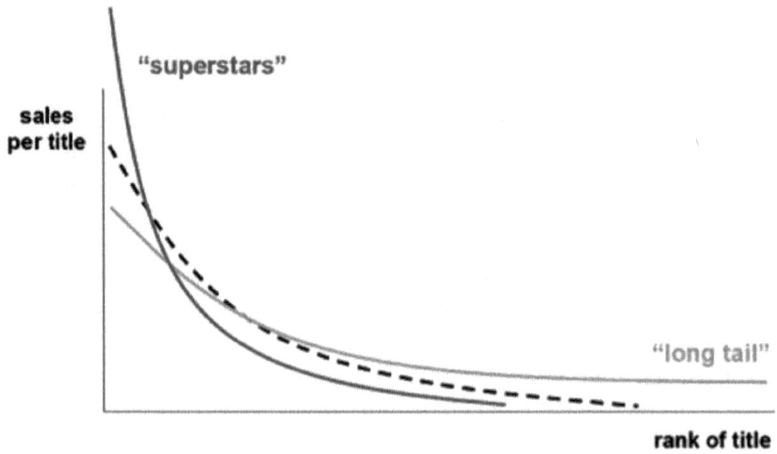

Fig. 8.2 Winner-take-all vs. The Long Tail

their investment, even at high rates of compensation for the superstar. However, if bands that are just starting out are able to get their music directly to the consumers without going through the record companies, both the musicians and the consumers will be better off.

8.7 "Winner-Take-All" Versus The Long Tail

The recorded music industry is still without question a winner-take-all industry where superstars like Johnny Cash and the Allman Brothers rule. The superstars vs. long tail effects are illustrated in Fig. 8.2. The superstars effect means that most of the recorded music sales are accounted for by records made by established artists. The Long Tail effect would imply that more record sales were by less well-known artists. Superstar artists still provide the most lucrative revenue streams for an ailing business. Observing the trends in the unit sales distribution over this 5-year period, a study by Strachan [131] provides support for the superstar effect and the "winner-take-all" view of the music industry. Though this research provides some support for the long tail effect, it is for non-digital sales which would appear to be somewhat at odds with the idea that the Internet and digital technology has enabled niche artists to increase their market share. Why then does the superstar effect continue in the industry today? Though there are undoubtedly varied answers, some conjectures can be made.

The fears that our music culture is being watered-down and homogenized by Internet technology and globalization are partially true. But this new technology and connectedness brings forth important benefits such as lower barriers to entry. The evidence Strachan finds for a long tail effect is not a dramatic erosion of the empires of the superstars, but more akin to a persistent "trickling down" of demand

Table 8.1 Top selling artists in sample, 2004–2008

Artist	Genre	First year on charts
Johnny Cash	Rockabilly, country, rock	1956
Allman Brothers Band	Rock	1971
Heart	Rock	1976
Chevelle	Rock	2002
Fiona Apple	Alternative pop-rock	1997
Don Williams	Country	1976
J. Holiday	R&B	2007
Wu-Tang Clan	Rap	1993

Source: [132]

towards indie artists. The indies most likely are using digital and Internet technology to connect with their indie fans, but the evidence of a long tail effect in recorded music sales is found in the physical and analog world. Indie fan loyalty and reciprocity may be expressed in buying CDs and LPs at shows and record stores. For many indie artists and fans, cultural relevancy is more important than commercial gains—at least on the surface [15, 16]. Although a long tail effect is observed, artists in the middle are not necessarily flourishing when it comes to record sales—perhaps they are losing the most in this situation.

As far as the superstars go, in the random sample used in Strachan's study for the period 2004–2008, the top selling artist each year by far was Johnny Cash who died in 2003. The other top sellers included the Allman Brothers Band, Heart, Chevelle, Fiona Apple, Don Williams, J. Holiday, and the Wu-Tang Clan. Table 8.1 provides a summary of the genre and first year on the charts for these artists.

Consider Johnny Cash who began his recording career at Sun Studios and was a member of what was later called "The Million Dollar Quartet"—Cash, Elvis Presley, Carl Perkins, and Jerry Lee Lewis. His biggest hits were "I Walk the Line" in 1956, then "Ring of Fire" in 1963, "A Boy Named Sue" in 1969, and "If I Were a Carpenter" in 1970. What did the songs have in common? They were all crossover hits in the country and pop genres. Cash became known as an "outlaw"—he used drugs and went to prison and in the late 60s recorded very successful albums at Folsom Prison and San Quentin. His last album was released in 2002 and included a cover version of the song "Hurt" by Nine Inch Nails and received popular and critical acclaim. Cash was always a rebel and this is what is most valued and rewarded in contemporary popular music.

The Allman Brothers Band, though formed more than four decades ago and with numerous personnel changes, remains a popular live performance group. They were inducted into the Rock and Roll Hall of Fame in 1995, and in November 2008, they received the Legend of Live Award from the *Billboard* Touring Awards. Heart is another group that has been around for four decades featuring the duo Nancy and Ann Wilson. They also are currently touring. The key to their success in selling records would appear to be both longevity, classic hits, and still on the road performing regularly.

The group Chevelle has been around for about a decade and has released several albums. Though originally signed to a Christian label, they are not a Christian rock band. Fiona Apple, a singer-songwriter, may have benefited from the fact that she sang a duet with Johnny Cash on his album *American IV: The Man Comes Around* in 2002 and was nominated for a Grammy award for a Grammy Award for "Best Country Collaboration with Vocals."

Don Williams is a singer-songwriter in the country music genre, though he was a member of the folk-pop group the Pozo-Seco Singers. In 2010, he was inducted into the Country Music Hall of Fame. He has had 17 number one hits and is still touring.

J. Holiday is a relatively new rap artist whose first appearance on the charts was with "Bed" which made the *Billboard* Hot 100 in 2007. He has a new album and is also touring. Wu-Tang Clan is a highly influential rap group whose individual members have gone on to solo careers. In 2007, MTV ranked Wu-Tang the fifth greatest hip-hop group of all time and About.com ranked them the number one greatest hip-hop group of all time.

In summary, this list of top selling artists in Strachan's sample indicate that the "superstar" effect is quite strong. However, what has kept artists like Johnny Cash on top is the fact that he created something new late in his career. It is unlikely that Cash would have continued to sell his old recordings without having made new recordings with popular current stars. Hence, there appears to be large returns to those incumbent artists who continue to innovate in their careers. Though most of the other artists in the list benefited from continued touring, Cash perhaps had some impact from the fact that he died in 2003 and posthumous albums and a movie were released. The key to more new music in the future is for both new and established musicians to continue to innovate and create new music and not rely on royalties from their back catalogues of recorded music.

Epilogue: Is Rock and Roll Here to Stay?

Technology has been both the source of the frequent rejuvenation of the industry while at the same time often threatening its long-term economic viability. The music business is undergoing revolutionary change due to the technology of the Internet. For most of the rock and roll era beginning in the mid-1950s, artists needed a record company to promote them and support their artistry. Today, there is some question whether record companies are needed at all. Artists are looking for new ways to promote themselves and their music. All sorts of ideas are being experimented with. Reggae fusion star Sean Kingston's album "Tomorrow" contained a special image that could be held up to a computer webcam to enable the fan to perform in a karaoke session on Kingston's Web site. The Beatles broke up more than four decades ago, yet their music has been remixed and used in a Cirque du Soleil show in Las Vegas.

Though a clichè, the only real constant in a dynamic society is change. In the process of change from the established way of life to something new, something old is necessarily destroyed. As I noted in the Prologue, the great economist Joseph Schumpeter stated that the essence of a capitalist or market economy was precisely this process of creative destruction. Those who bring new things, or innovations, to the marketplace are called entrepreneurs. Entrepreneurial activity has always driven the booms and busts of the music industry and today entrepreneurs in all facets of the music business—recording, performing, and distributing—are ushering in change in the music industry once again [113]. Especially in periods of great technological change and the disintegration of the accepted ways of business enterprise, it is the entrepreneur who is the progressive force that ultimately raises the standard of living of society as a whole. The entrepreneurs in the music industry include those who invented the electric guitar like Leo Fender and Adolph Rickenbacher, artists such as Elvis Presley and Buddy Holly who created new musical styles, those like Berry Gordy who founded Motown Records, and those who today are using digital technology and the Internet to bring more music to more people. The rise of the new entrepreneurship in music is promising that artists can potentially be better compensated than in the past.

R.J. Phillips, *Rock and Roll Fantasy?: The Reality of Going from Garage Band to Superstardom*, SpringerBriefs in Business 35, DOI 10.1007/978-1-4614-5900-2,

Music and Money

In 1972, the rock group Dr. Hook and the Medicine Show sang of their desire to get their picture on the "Cover of the Rolling Stone." In the 1960s, one important measure of success for artists was whether you got your picture on the cover of this leading music and cultural magazine that was founded in 1967. Mick Jagger and Keith Richards, the two most prominent members of The Rolling Stones, were on the cover of the magazine many times. However, three decades later Jagger and Richards were on the cover of *Fortune* magazine with a feature article titled "Inside Rock's Billion-Dollar Band" [127]. From the 1960s to the present day, there was a change in the focus of rock bands. The measure of "making it" in the rock and roll business went from being on the cover of a counterculture, politically left-wing leaning publication, to being on the cover of a magazine many view as a bastion of politically conservative free-market capitalism. In the 1960s, there was talk of groups "selling out"—creating music to make money instead of making music for cultural and "social consciousness" reasons. It was the era of the Vietnam war, civil rights, and women's liberation. Getting rich was not the "in" thing to do.

However, some people did get rich off music in the early days of rock and roll, and it typically wasn't the musician who wrote and performed the songs. Instead, it was the manager, the promoter, the music publisher, or the record company. Everyone is familiar with stories of artists who were not adequately compensated for their music or who lost royalty rights in questionable deals. From Little Richard to John Fogerty to The Beatles and The Rolling Stones—others profited from what the artists produced simply because of the outdated business model that distributed music revenue to those who did not really add value to the creation.

Contrast the experience of the early days of rock and roll with that of the rap and hip-hop artists like Jay-Z or 50 Cent. They not only write their songs, they perform them and record them, they distribute their music through their own record labels and even control merchandizing of all items related to their public image as an artist. The financial future of today's artists is more secure not only because they have both learned from the experience of earlier artists, but also because artists have become more involved in business decisions.

The Future of Music

Everybody loves to listen to music. Musicians love to create music. So why is the image of a "starving" musician so prevalent? The problem is that while musicians have been creative in their craft, too often their business affairs have been left to others. For one hundred years, the record companies enjoyed a business model that generated lots of revenue and paid lots of people very well. Most of those people were not performing musicians however. What we have now is a situation where technology is radically changing the relationship between those who have profited from the music industry who are not musicians and the performing musicians. This will require a fundamental change in the way of doing business. There is the possibility that in the future more of the revenue generated by the music industry will go to the musicians. The costs of operating the record business—the recording engineers, the music publishers, the A & R people, and countless others—will undergo a radical change due to the Internet and digital technology. This will also result in a period of great innovation in music as different musical styles and genres from many countries will become known by a larger audience.

Record company executives lament the fact that making a living from selling recorded music is a dying business. But in the past 200 years of American history, numerous industries have disappeared and countless jobs became obsolete. This is the situation that faces many in the recorded music industry. It is not that recording will disappear, it is just that musicians will have to rely on live performance, merchandizing, and new and creative ways to earn income from their music.

The record executives have also conveniently neglected two facts. First, musicians have always made their living primarily through live performance and secondarily by other means. Once upon a time, the sale of sheet music was an important source of income for musicians and it supported a very large industry and employed lots of people. Recorded music is going the way of sheet music. It will never go away, but it will not be the primary source of income. Indeed, for most musicians recorded music was never the primary source of income anyway.

The second fact that has been forgotten is that the separation of recording and playing music came only after the realization that selling recordings of established opera singers could be lucrative and because recording and record production technology required a complex and costly process.

This is no longer the case. Indeed, one wonders what the evolution of music in the twentieth century would have been like had phonographs continued to have the capability of recording and playing back as did the earliest cylinder phonographs. This was true of Thomas Edison's first phonograph in 1877, and though Edison thought his machine would have a business use, others realized that it could be used for home entertainment. But after others began to develop phonographs for entertainment, Edison's company also began to do so.

A magazine advertisement for an early Edison phonograph showed a family making a recording in their parlor: a woman at the piano, and a man and woman singing from sheet music into the large horn of the phonograph. Thus very early in the history of the phonograph it was promoted as a device that would bring the family together to produce music. Suppose that instead of the record companies dominating the production and consumption of music as they did in the twentieth century, everyone after 1900 had a home recorder. This was what was implied by the Edison phonograph advertising. Would we still have had great singers that dominated music consumption like Frank Sinatra and Elvis Presley, or instead would we have millions of people making and consuming their own music? This is the future that the record companies are afraid of.

Today, we have the possibility of actually realizing what was glimpsed for a short time in the early part of the twentieth century: not an industry of superstars, but rather one where everyone who wishes to produces and consumes his or her own music and then exchanges that music with others and even profit financially. Instead, we got a "winner-take-all" industry in which superstars made the money and not much was left for others. Will the Digital Age end this "winner-take-all" market structure in recorded music?

Making and distributing recorded music is now very cheap and hence the revenues it generates are declining. But it is still the case that you have to get your music heard. Traditionally this has been done through live performance, but today, with the Internet and digital technology, new possibilities are opening up for musicians. Live performance is financially very lucrative and touring is a booming business. The connection between live performance and the fans will become even closer in the future because it will be the key to making a living by performing music. Stated bluntly, the reality of the music industry today is that everyone whose income is dependent upon the sale of recorded music will see that income go to zero. These jobs are as obsolete and unneeded for the twenty-first century as the nineteenth century blacksmith was no longer needed for the age of the automobile in the twentieth. The blacksmith was replaced by the automobile mechanic and the music industry in the twenty-first century will witness similar transformations. *C'est la vie!* It is incredible to postulate the disappearance of an entire industry, but it has happened countless times before.

How is the Music Industry Changing?

Though the record companies are in trouble, the industry has always faced the problems of new technology and innovation in musical style and emerged with an even more pervasive role for music in society. Music is everywhere today and this is a result of the changes that technology and innovation have brought about.

To make it in the music industry today, not only do you have to be a creative musician, but you must also have business savvy for the Internet Age. You may have written a great song, but no one will ever hear it unless you get it on a commercial, a game, a movie, Internet radio, or a similar outlet. The old model where the record company invested heavily in publicity is defunct. Not only do the record companies often lack the funds to promote new acts, but also the sales of recordings are down, and hence the revenue flow is much lower. Record companies and artists must look for new ways to generate income if they wish to remain in the music industry.

Musicians have always had to innovate in order to be successful. Everyone has read stories about how the musicians in the 1950s and 1960s were ripped off—usually by their record companies, their manager, or their publishing company. John Fogerty for years refused to play his own songs because he had to give up royalties to Fantasy Records to get out of his contract while a member of Creedance Clearwater Revival in the 1960s. But today, one is more likely to hear stories of musicians getting millions of dollars for long-term contracts and of the income generated by their various entrepreneurial business ventures. Have musicians' fortunes really improved over the past fifty years? After all, Elvis Presley and The Beatles got rich. There is a crucial difference. Instead of the stories of artists being taken advantage in contracts that were signed when artists were new and unknown, today the multimillion-dollar contracts one hears about are deals by established artists. If the music industry is really better for the average musician, then what is crucial is whether the new, unknown artist has a better deal. Superstars always get good deals, even if they don't at first. Once they become established, they command bargaining power.

The reason early rock and roll artists signed bad contracts is because they were operating in an industry that was using business practices established at the turn of the twentieth century when recorded music was a new industry. It was monopoly power by the record companies and the high cost of recording that enabled this system to last for a hundred years. However, the digital and Internet revolution is now undermining that system. This is why the record companies fret over the demise of their industry. Their monopoly has been threatened.

Since at least medieval times when troubadours went from town to town singing their songs, musicians have earned their living through live performance. Should we be surprised that today the main way that virtually all musicians earn their living is through live performance? We are beginning to realize that the period of recorded music that dominated the twentieth century was in some measure a fluke. Buddy Holly and The Beatles dreamed of making their living solely from the sale of recorded music, but in fact, neither was able to do so and no one in the future will be able to do it at all.

Though established artists are getting multimillion-dollar deals, what about the new artist? This is where there has always been a problem. Because it is not known whether the public will like a new artist and his or her music, the record companies established a system that sought to minimize their risks and reduce potential losses. Recording and promoting an artist and his or her music was an expensive proposition. Today, with computers, recording can be very cheap. No longer is it necessary for a band to rent time at a recording studio. CDs or MP3s can be produced and distributed cheaply. What is different today is that the cost of producing and distributing music has fallen dramatically.

The problem with the old way of doing business in the music industry is that the record company had the upper hand in the contract with a new artist. Is there any way to make the contracts fairer for new artists? What is happening now is that we are moving toward a system that potentially can be better for new artists. New technology has finally enabled an entrepreneurial revolution in the standard business model in the music industry. However, the basic problem remains: How does a new artist find his or her audience? In the late nineteenth century when sheet music was the main source of income for songwriters and their publishers, it was through the song pluggers. In a market where the potential supply of songs exceeds the consumers' ability to listen to all of the music available, song pluggers were crucial. The same is true of DJs in the 1950s in the early days of rock and roll.

The record industry over a hundred-year period established a business model that was a shared monopoly. Record and then CD prices were essentially fixed by the record companies, and royalties were collected by ASCAP and later Broadcast

Music Incorporated (BMI) and enforced by the Recording Industry Association of America (RIAA). Each new recording and playback technology was greeted by the record industry as heralding the end of the music industry. This was true of reel-to-reel tape, cassettes, recordable CDs, and finally MP3s and other digital formats. The lobbyists for the recording industry have spent millions to protect the vested interests of the recording companies.

What will the Future be Like?

According to Steven Mithen in his book *The Singing Neanderthals,* humankind has been making music for thousands of years. Individuals have been earning a living from music for a much shorter period of time—perhaps a few hundred years [103]. Recorded music—the reproduction of a previously produced sound—is less than 150 years old [103]. The Age of Rock and Roll is less than 60 years old. Though technology has changed, what has not changed is the fundamental way in which a musician can be successful. You have to write a great song, you have to get that song heard by the public, and you have to make your living through performing live.

In the midst of one of the greatest technological revolutions in the history of humankind, and arguably the greatest dissemination of music on a global basis, the music industry finds itself in crisis. How will music continue if artists can no longer earn a living from selling recorded sound? The answer is that when viewed from a long perspective in human history, it should be no surprise that recorded music would never be a way to make a living in the long run. In fact, the period of time during which artists earned their living primarily by selling records is largely a fiction. The Beatles gave up live performance because to make live performance profitable in the 1960s, you needed better technology and larger and better venues. It was impossible for them to satisfy the enormous demand for their live performances without sacrificing quality (as in the concerts at Shea Stadium). But the result of giving up live performances was that the band eventually broke up. They made the attempt to return to live performance by making a movie—"Get Back," which ended with their impromptu live performance atop their recording studio in the middle of the day, in the midst of city crowds.

The reason that it appeared that making a living selling records was a viable alternative was because of the undeveloped nature of touring, especially in the 1950s and 1960s. Would The Rolling Stones ever consider giving up live performance and try to make a living from selling records? They never did, and now they never will.

Making a living from selling recorded sound is a small blip in the history of making music and earning a living from creating music. It lasted a hundred years because it was costly to create recorded sound and because record companies were able to adapt a business model that had been created prior to the era of recorded sound. It was the Tin Pan Alley business model combined with the recording studio that resulted in the modern era of recorded music. That era has now been eclipsed and we are returning to a time when musicians will make their living in many other ways, but not through selling prerecorded music as their major source of income. This does not mean that musicians will quit recording music. Indeed there will be even more recorded music; it is just that the price that consumers will pay for that commodity will tend to be zero. As the price falls to zero, consumer demand will increase. Musicians will keep supplying recorded music because it will enable them to earn an income from selling something else to the consumer at a positive price. As recorded music becomes free, the property rights associated with the creation of music will become irrelevant. It will not come back until that point in the future when the technology is available for one company to clone another company's "new Elvis."

Back to the Future?

My grandmother had a piano in her house. The only thing I remember her playing on it was "When the Roll is Called Up Yonder." I don't know if she ever had any formal music training and I don't know if she could read music. As far as I know she never owned a phonograph and did not listen to music on the radio but in later years, she probably watched the Lawrence Welk Show. But the fact is, as Elijah Wald noted in his recent book [144], over the course of the twentieth century, music evolved from something people produced themselves to people "consuming" music produced by others. As inventors refined and improved the technology and entrepreneurs and brought the technology to the mass of people at continually falling prices, the role of music in our society was transformed.

There has never been greater access to music than we are experiencing at the beginning of the twenty-first century. Music is seemingly everywhere from iPods to commercials to electronic games. But has this increase in quantity come at the expense of the quality of our music experience? Neil Young said in 2008 that the technology was ruining musical taste: "People's understanding of what's right and what's wrong or what's great and what's bad about music quality is totally skewed by the availability of MP3 and the acceptance of convenience."

John Philip Sousa and Neil Young agree: Technology is lowering the quality of the music experience for the average person. However, their comments are separated by a century—Sousa writing at the dawn of widely available recorded music and Young writing as digitally recorded music has become the standard. Is technology responsible for the decline in the quality of music? It's likely a number of music company executives would answer this question with a resounding "yes!"

Today, not only has technology enabled you to make music without any music knowledge or talent, but the listening experience has also been affected by the technology of MP3s. Neil Young stated that he first records his music with analog technology (magnetic recording tape) and then converts it to digital rather than going straight to digital because he likes the sound quality better than straight to digital. The late Steve Jobs, the cofounder of Apple, reportedly had a vacuum tube amplifier and vinyl albums for his music listening enjoyment. Could the Sousa and Young contentions be true that technology really brought us just bad music with bad sound? Could this be true at a time when the opportunity to hear the music of a very large and diverse group of musicians is seemingly unlimited?

It is not only the technology that has affected the quality and quantity of good music, but Sousa was also worried about the remuneration for composers of music. At the time he wrote his article in 1906, there were not many protections for composers of music. The Supreme Court had just ruled that the player piano technology was not a copyright violation. This meant that the makers of player pianos could use the music and sell their pianos without having to compensate the composers of the songs. Sousa asked why should songwriters keep writing songs? Gene Simmons of the 1970s rock band Kiss has blatantly stated that college students are destroying the music industry. This is in agreement with what Sousa said a century ago: there would no longer be an incentive to compose music and society as a whole will suffer. Was Sousa concerned about the state of musical expertise of the populace or was he really just worried that he wouldn't get compensated for his compositions when they were recorded? As it turned out, Congress passed the Copyright Act of 1909 and Sousa became a very popular recording artist. The band Kiss has done very well, and may someday make it into the Rock and Roll Hall of Fame.

From the earliest recorded cylinders to the latest digital encoding technology, the pervasiveness of music in our society has grown enormously and it is technology that made this possible. But the reason the technological change has been a boon to the industry is because individuals have brought the technology into commercial use so that more people can enjoy more and better music at a lower cost. There have also been innovations in musical styles from the Big Band to Elvis Presley through hip-hop.

Ironically, Schumpeter, like Karl Marx and Thorstein Veblen, was not optimistic about the future of capitalism because they all believed that large businesses would thwart the innovation of the entrepreneur. This description may have fit the music industry very well in early post-World War II period, but ultimately recording tape and musical innovation created the opportunity for independent artists to enter the music business. In the 1950s, the economist John Kenneth Gailbraith may have thought that technological innovation and the introduction of new goods would henceforth come from the large companies, but in music, those companies stagnated in the early 1950s just as they have stagnated today in the face of the Internet, digital technology, and innovations in music genres such as rap and hip-hop.

Modern-Day Flint Workers

Many years ago when I was an undergraduate, I read a parable about technological change and entrepreneurs as told by the great University of Texas economist Robert H. Montgomery. He wrote that one can imagine a million years ago when our forefathers were living in caves that someone chanced on a marvelous new substance which we now call bronze. He found that it could be molded and shaped into spear-heads, knives, and other tools. "We can get our food and clothing in less time. We can make our boats and houses better. We can overcome our enemies." Was he now a hero who received great acclaim? More likely he was tossed into the volcano. Why? Because there existed an Ancient and Honorable Order of Flint Workers. They owned the only good flint beds. They knew the art of chipping flint. They could protect the secrets of their craft and held positions of power and prestige and profit in the community. They did not like newfangled notions of bronze. But some of the tribesmen who had seen the bronze ax knew what it could do. So after a few generations and with the boldness and bravery of some youngster who opposed the Flint Workers, the Age of Bronze was born. So the Beaters of Bronze replaced the Flint Workers and, in turn, sought to establish a monopoly and to garner power and prestige. So it goes, Montgomery quips, for a half-million years or so [105]. Today, the record industry and all of its employees in all aspects of the way it operated throughout the twentieth century are the Ancient and Honorable Order of Flint Workers. How much longer can they maintain their old ways of doing business? It depends upon the development of new technologies and the inventive efforts of entrepreneurs in the music industry.

Rock and roll music has confounded the many predictions of its imminent demise. It emerged in the post-World War II era as the music of those who were in their teen years. Like other industries, it had an initial period characterized by innovation by small firms, and now has evolved into a mature industry that is dominated by large firms. However, technology has allowed innovation to continue in rock and roll music. No one can predict the demise of a music genre, but rock and roll has proven to be very resilient. This does not mean that the music has been stagnant. Much has changed from its early roots in gospel and blues, though it remains at its core a music form embraced by youth.

There are interesting developments that are likely to impact the future evolution of rock and roll. One is the substitution of capital for labor in the production of music. Software programs are available today that allow virtually anyone, regardless of their musical training or skill, to compose music. The rap and hip-hop DJs who sample music recordings are but one form of the new music composer. We will perhaps reach a point where everyone can create his or her own music. Far from decreasing the demand for music, this development is likely to increase the prominence of music. Indeed, it may also be the case that the expansion of the new music industry will usher in an era of increased economic development in cities [55, 56, 116].

The same can be said for the Internet. Those who thought it would lead to a decline in revenues and therefore the disappearance of artists have had to recognize that, in fact, the Internet has stimulated the demand for music. Bootlegs of recorded music have been around for a long time, yet there is no evidence that it decreases the overall demand for music in the long run. The key for the music industry, as with every industry in a market economy, is innovation in the product offered to the consumer. Those industries that do not innovate, or that ineffectively compete with other similar products, will decline. The same is true for rock and roll.

References

1. *Dravs drives demand for producer-writers with new creative venture.*, Music Week (2011), no. 36, 12.
2. Peter J. Alexander, *Entropy and popular culture: Product diversity in the popular music recording industry*, American Sociological Review 61 (1996), 171 –74.
3. Ellis Amburn, *Buddy holly: A biography*, St. Martin's Press, New York, 1995.
4. Birgitte Andersen, Richard Kozul Wright, and Zeljka Kozul Wright, *Rents, rights n'rhythm: Cooperation, conflict and capabilities in the music industry*, Industry and Innovation 14 (2007), no. 5, 513540.
5. Chris Anderson, *The long tail: Why the future of business is selling less of more*, Hyperion, New York, 2008.
6. History Department at the University of San Diego, *Yankee doodle*, (accessed March 2009).
7. David Audretsch, *The entrepreneurial society*, Oxford University Press, New York, 2007.
8. David B. Audretsch, *Joseph schumpeter and john kenneth galbraith: 2 sides of the same coin*, Indiana University, March 2008.
9. Alan J. Baker, *A model of competition and monopoly in the record industry*, Journal of Cultural Economics 15 (1991), no. 1, 29–54.
10. William J. Baumol, *The free-market innovation machine: Analyzing the growth miracle of capitalism*, Princeton University Press, Princeton, 2002.
11. William J. Baumol and William G. Bowen, *Performing arts—the economic dilemma*, Twentieth Century Fund, New York, 1966.
12. Mark A. Bellis, Tom Hennell, Clare Lushey, Karen Hughes, Karen Tocque, and John R Ashton, *Elvis to Eminem: quantifying the price of fame through early mortality of European and North American rock and pop stars*, Journal of Epidemiological Community Health 61 (2007), 896901, doi: 10.1136/jech.2007.059915.
13. David Blackburn, *On-line piracy and recorded music sales*, unpublished, December 2004.
14. Hank Bordowitz, *Dirty little secrets of the record business*, Chicago Review Press, Chicago, 2007.
15. Pierre Bourdieu, *Distinction: A social critique of the judgment of taste*, Harvard University Press, Cambridge, MA, 1984.
16. ____________, *The field of cultural production*, Columbia University Press, New York, 1993.
17. Simon Bowmaker (ed.), *Economics uncut: A complete guide to life, death and misadventure*, Edward Elgar, Cheltenham, U.K, 2005.
18. Simon W. Bowmaker, Ronnie J. Phillips, and Richard D. Johnson, *Economics of rock 'n' roll.*, pp. 389–421, Cheltenham, U.K. and Northampton, Mass: U Edinburgh, 2005.

R.J. Phillips, *Rock and Roll Fantasy?: The Reality of Going from Garage Band to Superstardom*, SpringerBriefs in Business 35, DOI 10.1007/978-1-4614-5900-2,

19. Erik Brynjolfsson, Yu Hu, and Duncan Simester, *Goodbye pareto principle, hello long tail: The effect of search costs on the concentration of product sales*, MIT Center for eBusiness, 2006.
20. Andrew E. Burke, *The dynamics of product differentiation in the British record industry*, Journal of Cultural Economics 20 (1996a), 145–164.
21. ___________, *How effective are international copyright conventions in the music industry?*, Journal of Cultural Economics 20 (1996b), 51–66.
22. ___________, *Small firm start–up by composers in the recording industry*, Small Business Economics 9 (1997), 463–471.
23. ___________, *Music business*, A Handbook of Cultural Economics (Ruth Towse, ed.), Edward Elgar, Cheltenham, UK & Northampton, MA, 2003, p. xxx.
24. Samuel Cameron, *Rock, pop and judicial efficiency: Economic considerations in the spandau ballet decisions*, Journal of Interdisciplinary Economics 17 (2006), no. 3, 327–344.
25. Samuel Cameron and Alan Collins, *Transaction costs and partnerships: The case of rock bands*, Journal of Economic Behavior and Organization 32 (1997), 171–183.
26. David E. Cavazos and Dara Szyliowicz, *How industry associations suppress threatening innovation: The case of the US recording industry.*, Technology Analysis and Strategic Management 23 (2011), no. 5, 473–487.
27. Richard Caves, *Creative industries: Contracts between art and commerce*, Harvard University Press, Cambridge, 2000.
28. CBSNEWS.com, *Tower records files for bankruptcy*, 2004.
29. Steve Chapple and Reebee Garofalo, *Rock and roll is here to pay: The history and politics of the music industry*, Nelson-Hall, Chicago, 1977.
30. Eric Chiang and Djeto Assane, *Determinants of music copyright violations on the university campus*, Journal of Cultural Economics 31 (2007), 187–204, 10.1007/s10824-007-9042-y.
31. Eric P. Chiang and Djeto Assane, *Estimating the willingness to pay for digital music*, Contemporary Economic Policy, Vol. 27, No. 4, pp. 512–522, October 2009.
32. Ed Christman, *Stormy weather*, Billboard (2009), xxx.
33. ___________, *Turning publishing upside down*, Billboard (2012), 19–21.
34. Cinzia Ciardi and Alessandro Balestrino, *'I Wish Someone Help Me Write this Song'; Or, the Efficient Allocation of Resources in Rock Bands*, SSRN eLibrary (2010).
35. R. H. Coase, *Payola in radio and television broadcasting*, Journal of Law and Economics 22 (1979), no. 2, 269–328.
36. Carl M. Colonna, Patricia M. Kearns, and John E. Anderson, *Electronically produced music and its economic effects on the performing musician and music industry*, Journal of Cultural Economics 17 (1993), no. 2, 69–75.
37. Marie Connolly and Alan B. Krueger, *Chapter 20 rockonomics: The economics of popular music*, Handbook on the Economics of Art and Culture, vol. 1, Elsevier, 2006, pp. 667–719.
38. Tyler Cowen, *Why I do not believe in the cost disease: A comment on baumol*, Journal of Cultural Economics 20 (1996), 207–214.
39. ___________, *In praise of commercial culture*, Harvard University Press, Cambridge, 1998.
40. ___________, *Creative destruction: How globalization is changing the worlds cultures*, Princeton University Press, Princeton, N.J., 2002.
41. ___________, *Good and plenty: The creative successes of American arts funding*, Princeton, 2006.
42. W. Mark Crain and Robert D. Tollison, *Consumer choice and the popular music industry: A test of the superstar theory*, Empirica 29 (2002), 1–9, 10.1023/A:1014651130414.
43. William Crain and Robert D. Tollison, *Economics and the architecture of popular music*, Journal of Economic Behavior and Organization 901 (1997), 185–205.
44. Mark Cunningham, *Good vibrations: A history of record production*, Sanctuary Publishing Ltd., London, 1998.
45. Nicolas Curien and Fraçois Moreau, *The music industry in the digital era: Toward new contracts*, Journal of Media Economics 22 (2009), 102113.

46. Frederic Dannen, *Hit men: Power brokers and fast money inside the music business*, Vintage Books, New York, 1991.
47. Matthew David, *Peer to peer and the music industry: The criminalization of sharing*, Sage, Los Angeles, 2010.
48. Juan de Montoro Pons and Manuel Cuadrado Garca, *Legal origin and intellectual property rights: an empirical study in the prerecorded music sector*, European Journal of Law and Economics 26 (2008), 153–173, 10.1007/s10657-008-9056-8.
49. Jon Donlon and et. al., *The twenty biggest record-company screw-ups ever*, Blender (2008), 56–60.
50. Nicholsas Economides, *The economics of networks.*, International Journal of Industrial Organization 14, no. 2.
51. Michael A. Einhorn, *Transactions Costs and Administered Markets: License Contracts for Music Performance Rights*, Review of Economic Research on Copyright Issues, Vol. 3, No. 1, pp. 61–74, 2006.
52. Anita Elberse, *Bye bye bundles: The impact of the unbundling of music in digital channels*, (2009).
53. Anita Elberse and Felix Oberholzer-Gee, *Superstars and underdogs: An examination of the long-tail phenomenon in video sales*, July 2008.
54. Marc Eliot, *Rockonomics: The money behind the music*, Citadel Press, New York, 1993.
55. Richard Florida and Scott Jackson, *Sonic city: The evolving economic geography of the music industry*, 29 (2010), no. 3, 310–321.
56. Richard Florida, Charlotta Mellander, and Kevin Stolarick, *Music scenes to music clusters: The economic geography of music in the US, 1970–2000.*, Environment and Planning A 42 (2010), no. 4, 785–804.
57. Ben Fong-Torres, *Hickory wind: The life and times of gram parsons*, Pocket Books, New York, 1991.
58. Pete Frame, *Rock family trees*, Omnibus Press, London, 1993.
59. Robert H. Frank and Peter J. Cook, *The winner-take-all society: Why the few at the top get so much more than the rest of us*, Penguin Books, New York, 1995.
60. Jeffrey L. Funk, *Technological change within hierarchies: The case of the music industry*, Economics of Innovation and New Technology 16 (2007), no. 1, 1–16.
61. David Galenson, *From 'white christmas' to sgt. pepper: The conceptual revolution in popular music*, 2007, Working Paper 13308.
62. Terrel Galloway and Douglas Kinnear, *Unchained melody: A price-discrimination-based policy proposal for addressing the mp3 revolution*, Journal of Economic Issues (2001), 279–287.
63. Nelson George, *Hip hop America*, Penguin Books, New York, 1998.
64. David E. Giles, *Increasing returns to information in the US popular music industry*, Applied Economics Letters 14 (2007), no. 5–6, 327–331.
65. David E. Giles, *Superstardom in the US popular music industry revisited*, Economics Letters 92 (2006), no. 1, 68–74.
66. ___________, *Survival of the hippest: life at the top of the hot 100*, Applied Economics 39 (2007).
67. Charlie Gillet, *The sound of the city: The rise of rock and roll*, Da Capo Press, New York, 1996.
68. Isaac Goldberg and George Gershwin, *Tin pan alley: A chronicle of the American popular music racket*, The John Day Company, New York, 1930.
69. John Goldrosen and John Beecher, *Remembering buddy: The definitive biography*, Da Capo Press, New York, 1996.
70. Lee Gomes, *Many companies still cling to big hits to drive earnings*, Wall Street Journal (2006), Eastern Edition, August 2.
71. Fred Goodman, *The mansion on the hill: Dylan, young, Geffen, Springsteen, and the head-on collision of rock and commerce*, Times Books, New York, 1997.

72. Terry Gourvish and Kevin Tennent, *Peterson and berger revisited: Changing market dominance in the british popular music industry, c.1950–80.*, Business History 52 (2010), no. 2, 187–206.
73. Angela Harris, *History of the United States national anthem the star-spangled banner*, June 2009.
74. Clinton Heylin, *Bootleg: The secret history of the other recording industry*, St. Martin's Griffin, New York, 1996.
75. Jens Leth Hougaard and Mich Tvede, *Selling digital music: Business models for public goods.*, Netnomics 11 (2010), no. 1, 85–102.
76. James Hubbart, *Publics veto power over music missing*, Los Angeles Times (1961).
77. Kai-Lung Hui and Ivan Png, *Piracy and the legitimate demand for recorded music*, Contributions to Economic Analysis and Policy 2 (2003), no. 1, 1–22.
78. IFPI, *The recording industry commerical piracy report*, 2003.
79. Adrian Johns, *Death of a pirate: British radio and the making of the information age*, W. W. Norton and Co., New York, 2011.
80. William R. Johnson, *The economics of copying*, Journal of Political Economy 93 (1985), no. 1, 158–174.
81. Steve Jones, *The cassette underground*, Autonomedia.
82. Peter Kafka and Kemp Powers., *The road to riches.*, Forbes 172 (2003), no. 1, 78–82.
83. Ariel Katz, *The potential demise of another natural monopoly: Rethinking the collective administration of performing rights*, Journal of Competition Law and Economics 1 (2005), no. 3.
84. ___________, *The potential demise of another natural monopoly: New technologies and the administration of performing rights*, Journal of Competition Law and Economics 2 (2006), no. 2.
85. Barry Kernfeld, *Pop song piracy: Disobedient music distribution since 1929*, University of Chicago Press, Chicago, 2011.
86. Christopher C. Klein and Shea W. Slonaker, *Chart turnover and sales in the recorded music industry: 1990–2005.*, Review of Industrial Organization 36 (2010), no. 4, 351–372.
87. Amy E. Knaup and Merissa C. Piazza, *Business employment dynamics data: survival and longevity, ii*, Monthly Labor Review (2007), 3–10.
88. Steve Knopper, *Appetite for self-destruction: The spectacular crash of the record industry in the digital age*, Free Press, New York, 2009.
89. Greg Kot, *Ripped—how the wired generation revolutionized music*, Scribner, New York, 2009.
90. Roland J. Kushner and Arthur C. Brooks, *The one-man band by the quick lunch stand: Modeling audience response to street performance*, Journal of Cultural Economics 24 (2000), 65–77, 10.1023/A:1007585518269.
91. Larry Lehmer, *The day the music died: The last tour of buddy holly, the big bopper and ritchie valens*, Schirmer Books, New York, 1997.
92. Devin Leonard, *Songs in the key of Steve*, Fortune 147 (2003), no. 9, 00158259.
93. Daniel J. Levitin, *This is your brain on music: The science of a human obsession*, Plume Books, New York, 2006.
94. Peter Lewis, *Plug in, turn on, tune up*, Fortune 149 (2004), no. 4.
95. Stan Liebowitz, *The impact of reprography on the copyright system*, 1981, Revision Studies. Bureau of Corporate Affairs.
96. ___________, *Policing pirates in the networked age*, Policy Analysis (2002), no. 438, Washington, DC: The Cato Institute.
97. ___________, *Will mp3 downloads annihilate the record industry: The evidence so far*, 2003, Department of Management, The University of Texas at Dallas.
98. Guy Logsdon, *The flip of a coin: The story of tommy allsup with buddy holly, bob wills and other music legends*, Guy Logsdon Books, Tulsa, Oklahoma, 2011.
99. Paul D Lopes, *Innovation and diversity in the popular music industry, 1969 to 1990*, American Sociological Review 57 (1992), no. 1, 56–71.
100. Dave Marsh, *Louie Louie*, Hyperion, New York, 1993.
101. Michael Masnick and Dennis Yang, *Brainstorming session on new business models for the music industry report: From theory to action*, 2011, Floor64, Inc.

102. John Mellancamp, *On my mind: The state of the music business*, March 22 2009, (accessed in March 2009).
103. Steven Mithen, *The singing Neanderthals: The origins of music, language, mind, and body*, Harvard University Press, Cambridge, Mass., 2006.
104. Joeri M. Mol and Nachoem M. Wijnberg, *Competition, selection and rock and roll: The economics of payola and authenticity*, Journal of Economic Issues (2007), 701–714.
105. Robert H. Montgomery, *The brimstone game*, Viking, New York, 1940.
106. Abhinay Muthoo, *Bargaining Theory and Royalty Contract Negotiations*, Review of Economic Research on Copyright Issues, Vol. 3, No. 1, pp. 19–27, 2006.
107. Alireza Jay Naghavi and Günther G. Schulze, *Bootlegging in the music industry*, 2000.
108. Richard Neer, *Fm: The rise and fall of rock radio*, Villard, New York, NY, 2001.
109. Philip Norman, *Rave on: The biography of buddy holly*, Simon and Schuster, New York, 1996.
110. Will Page and Eric Garland, *The long tail of p2p*, PRS for Music (2009), no. 14, 1–8.
111. William Patry, *Moral panics: The copyright wars*, Oxford University Press, Oxford, 2009.
112. Richard A. Peterson, *Why 1955? explaining the advent of rock music*, Popular Music 9 (1990), no. 1.
113. Richard A. Peterson and David G. Berger, *Entrepreneurship in organizations: evidence from the popular music industry*, Administrative Science Quarterly 16 (1971), 97–107.
114. ____________, *Cycles in symbol production: The case of popular music*, American Sociological Review 40 (1975), no. 2, 158–173.
115. Richard A. Peterson and David G. Berger, *Measuring industry concentration, diversity, and innovation in popular music*, American Sociological Review 61 (1996), no. 1, 175–178.
116. Ronnie J. Phillips, *Arts entrepreneurship and economic development: Can every city be 'austintatious'?*, Foundations and Trends in Entrepreneurship 6 (2010), no. 4, 239–313.
117. Ivan L. Pitt, *Superstar effects on royalty income in a performing rights organization.*, Journal of Cultural Economics 34 (2010), no. 3, 219–236.
118. Oliver Read and Walter L. Welch, *From tin foil to stereo: Evolution of the phonograph*, Howard W. Sams & Co., Indianapolis, Indiana, 1959 (1976).
119. RIAA, *Recording industry association of America consumer profile*, 2002.
120. Joan Robinson, *The economics of imperfect competition*, 2 ed., St. Martin's Press, London, 1969.
121. J. Rogan, *Timeless flight: The definitive biography of the byrds*, Scorpion/Dark Star, London, 1981.
122. Sherwin Rosen, *The economics of superstars*, The American Economic Review 71 (1981), no. 5, 845–858.
123. E. Samuels, *The illustrated story of copyright*, Thomas Dunne Books, New York, 2000.
124. F. M. Schrer, *Quarter notes and bank notes: The economics of music composition in the eighteenth and nineteenth centuries*, Princeton University Press, Princeton, N.J., 2004.
125. Joseph A. Schumpeter, *Capitalism, socialism, and democracy*, HarperPerennial, New York, 1942.
126. Kerry Segrave, *Payola in the music industry: A history, 1880–1991*, McFarland and Company, Jefferson, North Carolina, 1994.
127. Andy Serwer, Julia Boorstin, and Ann Harrington, *Inside the rolling stones inc.*, Fortune 146 (2002), no. 6.
128. David Sköld and Alf Rehn, *Makin' it, by keeping it real: Street talk, rap music, and the forgotten entrepreneurship from 'the 'hood'*, Group & Organization Management 32 (2007), no. 1, 50–78.
129. Richard R. Smith, *The history of rickenbacker guitars*, Centerstream Publishing, Fullerton, CA, 1987.
130. Brian Southhall and Rupert Perry, *Northern songs: The true story of the beatles song publishing empire*, Omnibus Press, London, 2006.
131. Ian Strachan, *The end of the winner-take-all society? property rights and the economics of the long tail in the music industry*, Ph.D. thesis.

132. Eric A. Strobl and Clive Tucker, *The dynamics of chart success in the U.K. pre-recorded popular music industry*, Journal of Cultural Economics 24 (2000), 113–134.
133. Joe Stuessy and Scott Lipscomb, *Rock and roll: Its history and stylistic development*, 6 ed., Prentice-Hall, Upper Saddle River, New Jersey, 2009.
134. Lisa Takeyama, *The welfare implications of unauthorized reproduction of intellectual property in the presence of demand network externalities*, Journal of Industrial Economics 42 (1994), no. 2, 155–166.
135. Los Angeles Times, *Ex-disc jockey reveals 2-year $15,500 payola.*
136. ____________, *How come payola? well thats show biz*, December 1959.
137. ____________, *Phony ratings, payoffs rapped by disc jockey*, (1959).
138. ____________, *Record promoter says he, others rigged lists of alleged hit discs*, (1960).
139. The New York Times, *Dramatic authors ask for protection*, The New York Times (1908).
140. Pete Townshend, *John peel lecture*, November 2011.
141. Paul Trynka (ed.), *Rock hardware: Forty years of rock instrumentation*, Balafon Books, London, 1996.
142. Peter Tschmuck, *Creativity and innovation in the music industry.*
143. Hal R. Varian, *Copying and copyright*, The Journal of Economic Perspectives 19 (2005), no. 2, 121–138.
144. Elijah Wald, *How the beatles destroyed rock n roll*, Oxford University Press, New York, 2009.
145. Joel Waldfogel, *Bye, bye, miss American pie? the supply of new recorded music since napster*, Working Paper 16882, National Bureau of Economic Research, March 2011.
146. James L. Walker, *This business of urban music*, Billboard Books, New York, 2008.
147. Richard Watt, *Licensing and Royalty Contracts for Copyright*, Review of Economic Research on Copyright Issues, Vol. 3, No. 1, pp. 1–17, 2006.
148. Heidi Westerlund, *Garage rock bands: A future model for developing musical expertise?*, International Journal of Music Education 24 (2006), no. 3, 119–125.
149. Joel Whitburn, *A century of pop music*, Record Research, Inc., Menomonee Falls, Wisconsin, 1999.
150. ____________, *Billboard pop hits singles and albums, 1940–1954*, Record Research, Inc., Menomonee Falls, Wisconsin, 2002.
151. ____________, *The billboard albums, 1956–2005*, 6th ed., Record Research, Inc., Menomonee Falls, Wisconsin, 2006a.
152. ____________, *Top Pop, Singles, 1955–2006*, Record Research, Inc., Menomonee Falls, Wisconsin, 2007.
153. ____________, *The billboard hot 100 annual, 1955–2005*, 7 ed., Record Research, Inc., Menomonee Falls, Wisconsin, 2006.
154. Forrest White, *Fender: The inside story*, Backbeat Books, San Francisco, 1994.
155. Steven S. Wildman, *An economic analysis of recording contracts*, A study funded by the Recording Industry Association of America, 2002.
156. Robert Yuyuenyongwatana, Aubree Helvey, and Jim Horner, *The evolution of copyright issues in music: From little cotton dolly to ol dirty bastard*, 2006.
157. Frank Zappa and Peter Occhiogrosso, *The real frank zappa book*, Poseidon Press., New York, 1989.

Song Index

R.J. Phillips, *Rock and Roll Fantasy?: The Reality of Going from Garage Band to Superstardom*, SpringerBriefs in Business 35, DOI 10.1007/978-1-4614-5900-2,

Subject Index

R.J. Phillips, *Rock and Roll Fantasy?: The Reality of Going from Garage Band to Superstardom*, SpringerBriefs in Business 35, DOI 10.1007/978-1-4614-5900-2,

MIX
Papier aus verantwortungsvollen Quellen
Paper from responsible sources
FSC® C105338

If you have any concerns about our products,
you can contact us on
ProductSafety@springernature.com

In case Publisher is established outside the EU,
the EU authorized representative is:
Springer Nature Customer Service Center GmbH
Europaplatz 3, 69115 Heidelberg, Germany

Printed by Libri Plureos GmbH
in Hamburg, Germany